Contents

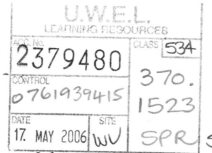

Marilee Sprenger

CORWIN PRESS, INC.
A Sage Publications Company
Thousand Oaks, California

For information:

Corwin Press, Inc.
A Sage Publications Company
2455 Teller Road
Thousand Oaks, California 91320
www.corwinpress.com

Sage Publications Ltd.
6 Bonhill Street
London EC2A 4PU
United Kingdom

Sage Publications India Pvt. Ltd.
B-42, Panchsheel Enclave
Post Box 4109
New Delhi 110 017 India

Printed in the United States of America

Library of Congress Cataloging-in-Publication Data

Sprenger, Marilee, 1949-
Differentiation through learning styles and memory / Marilee Sprenger.
    p. cm.
Includes bibliographical references and index.
ISBN 0-7619-3941-5 (cloth) — ISBN 0-7619-3942-3 (paper)
  1. Learning. 2. Memory. 3. Brain. I. Title.
LB1060.S695 2003
370.15′23—dc21

                           2003001244

05   06   10 9 8 7 6 5 4 3

Acquisitions Editor:	Robert D. Clouse
Associate Editor:	Kristen L. Gibson
Editorial Assistants:	Erin Clow/Jingle Vea
Production Editor:	Melanie Birdsall
Copy Editor:	Teresa Herlinger
Typesetter:	C&M Digitals (P) Ltd.
Proofreader:	Kristin Bergstad
Indexer:	Kathy Paparchontis
Cover Designer:	Tracy E. Miller
Production Artist:	Lisa Miller

Acknowledgments

There are many outstanding professional researchers, speakers, and trainers who influenced this book. Daniel Goleman, Carol Ann Tomlinson, Dawna Markova, Michael Grinder, and Mel Levine are a few who have provided information and strategies that have helped me in my classroom and my personal life. The memory researchers continually amaze me as they unravel the mysteries of the brain. Listening to and speaking with Dan Schacter, Kenneth Kosik, Bruce McEwen, and Steve Peterson, to name just a few, has been enlightening and gratifying.

There are others to whom I am grateful. First, I must thank Margo, for without her inspiration, this book would not have been possible. My colleagues at Two Rivers Professional Development Center guided this journey. Nancy Hinnen and Jan Leonard pursued their own path toward differentiation, and brainstorming with them helped me put my approach in perspective. Dr. Sally Weber, our director, gave me the support and flexibility to get the book completed. A very special thanks goes to my friend and associate Gail Owen, who read, questioned, and encouraged the submission of the manuscript.

This book is dedicated to my husband, Scott, for his unconditional love and support, and to the two most wonderful children in the world, Josh and Marnie. They have always been the source of my understanding of the need for differentiation: Josh, who knew how to play the game, and Marnie, who had to make up her own. Differentiated classrooms would have made education more rewarding for each of them.

About the Author

Marilee Sprenger is a creative and compassionate educator who interprets and applies current brain research for classroom practice. She is an experienced classroom teacher at the elementary, middle school, high school, and university levels. As an independent consultant, her passion is brain-based teaching and best practices using brain research and differentiation. She also consults in the areas of learning styles, using music in the classroom, teaming, multiple intelligences, emotional intelligence, and memory. As an educational consultant with Two Rivers Professional Development Center, she works for the Illinois Regional Offices of Education in the area of staff development associated with learning standards and testing. She speaks internationally, and her interactive and engaging style allows participants the opportunity to make connections to their classrooms and their students. She is affiliated with the American Academy of Neurology and is constantly updated on current research. Marilee is the author of several books including *Learning and Memory: The Brain in Action*, published by the Association for Supervision and Curriculum Development (ASCD), and *Becoming a Wiz at Brain-Based Teaching*, published by Corwin Press. She has published numerous articles, including "Memory Lane Is a Two-Way Street" in *Educational Leadership* and "The Sensational Classroom" in the *ASCD Brain-based Education/Learning Styles Networker*. Her dedication to education has won her many awards, but she cherishes most the wonderful students and teachers whose lives have touched hers. At her schools she was always the "brainlady," a nickname she lives up to. Marilee may be reached at 5820 Briarwood Lane, Peoria, Illinois, 61614; by calling (309) 692–5820; and by email at msprenge@aol.com. Her Web site is www.brainlady.com.

Prologue

Margo and I are in the teacher's lounge grabbing a cup of coffee before our prep period is over. We have been working on the school newspaper, and as usual, there are many changes to make before Friday's deadline.

Janice, our new fourth-grade teacher, comes into the room and is visibly shaken.

She blurts out, "I don't know what I'm going to do with those kids. I teach and teach and nothing seems to work! I stay up late working on my lesson plans. They're organized. They're complete. They're at grade level. They're just like the ones I designed in my college classes. It's got to be these kids, or maybe I'm not cut out for this job."

Her tears start to fall. It's 1994 and I quickly think back to when I took my position in 1989. There were many nights I walked out of here in tears. It took three years, much research, and several classes for me to get it figured out. Margo and I had spent many evenings on the phone talking things through. Our classes in this school were so diverse—much more so than my classes seemed in the seventies and the early eighties. What were the differences?

I return to the present. "Okay, Janice, we need to sit down and talk. Margo and I have worked on this problem for years, and we've figured a few things out. There are some strategies that we can share with you. It's a bit different in the real world than in those college classes. And we have a very unique situation here. We're an inner-city parochial school. That means we have a very diverse population. We have students who have been expelled from public schools. They are behavior problems, and many of them became behavior problems because they weren't academically successful. We have students who come from generational poverty, and we have students whose parents did not want them labeled 'special education,' so they brought them here where we don't have the special classes. We have kids whose parents are divorced or separated. They share custody, and sometimes these kids don't know whose house they'll be sleeping at. They often don't have homework and supplies for that reason. On top of that, we have the middle-of-the-road kids and some very gifted children. Is it any wonder that your one-size-fits-all lesson plans aren't working for everyone?"

Margo nods in agreement and says, "Janice, pull yourself together and act confident. We'll walk you through this. You're looking at forty years of experience between the two of us. We can probably make your classroom more fun for you and the kids, too."

Janice smiles and wipes her tears. "Thanks, this really means a lot to me."

"Don't give it a second thought," Margo replies. "Your students will be our students next year—we want them coming to us with a solid background. Our future is at stake here, too!"

We arranged for Janice to observe several of our classes. She took lots of notes, asked lots of questions, and kept saying, "You do things so differently than I do. Why do you do things that way? Why are those kids working together? And why is she working alone? Are they all working on the same stuff? You have learning centers in the upper grades? Aren't those just for primary kids?"

THE WAY WE DO THE THINGS WE DO

Margo always had better discipline than I did. I envied her power and control. And her students loved her for her consistency and kindness. She was already at the school when I joined the faculty. The "classroom from hell" was mine, but once a day Margo had my kids. She controlled them, while I had a terrible time. When I started doing research and applying it, I saw a difference in the way my classroom ran. When I used some brain-compatible strategies, the students began to change. They started learning. Margo became curious, took some of the same classes I had taken, watched what I was doing, and started applying some of the same techniques. She still had power and control, but the kids were learning more than ever before.

It wasn't enough, though. We realized that there had to be more instructional strategies and theories that successful teachers were using.

Margo took a workshop day and visited other schools. She returned with more information. We walked into the teacher's lounge each day smiling. We shared what we were planning, gave each other suggestions, and re-grouped when necessary.

We were happy because we had a plan. The plan was simple: Keep things moving, teach in a variety of ways, let kids teach each other, help kids feel like they belong, and when things don't work—try a different approach. You can't expect to teach in the same way and get different results.

We were making some changes with content, but mostly we were making instructional changes. We also changed assessment methods. We wanted our students to be involved with their learning and have the ability to share that learning in a comfortable style. We still had standard paper-and-pencil assessments, but we knew we had to prepare our students for those in an atypical way.

We were differentiating, but we didn't know it. We were designing rubrics, but we didn't know that either. What *did* we think we were doing? Surviving. Helping kids. Making sense of what we were doing. And having fun along the way.

Environments for Learning 1

"There's something different about your classroom," Janice announces one day in the lunchroom.

"What do you mean?" Margo asks.

"There's just a different feeling in there," she replies. "What do you do to make it different?"

"Different from yours or different from everybody's?" I coach Janice as I look at Margo.

"Yours is different from Margo's, but in a way, it's the same. I just know that my classroom is not like either of yours. What do you do to make it like that? The kids act so differently in your rooms," she relates.

Margo pipes up, "We do brain-based teaching. Our classrooms are brain-compatible. That means we follow some basic principles. The students are more relaxed and more learning takes place."

"So, is brain-based teaching the same as differentiation?" Janice inquires.

"Many of the principles of differentiation and brain-based teaching rest on the same foundations. Good teaching practices are good teaching practices. They both lend themselves to student-centered classrooms. That's what you're seeing and feeling that is different in our rooms. We center the learning experiences around the students instead of around us," I suggest.

"Well, my classroom isn't anything like that. There are so many things I think I have to tell the students. If I don't, how will they ever learn it?" she sighs.

Margo tells her, "I went to a workshop about basic presentation skills given by Bob Pike (1994). I was told that as teachers and

1

trainers, we spend way too much time trying to get our learners to know everything. That's totally unnecessary. Just as the students have to decide what is most important to study and learn, we have to decide what they need to know—then if there is time, we give them the stuff that is nice to know!"

"Please, start at the beginning," Janice asks. "Your rooms are interesting. The students seem to know exactly what to do, and there's no tension. What do I need to do first?" She sits quietly and waits for us to begin.

A PLACE TO START

The process of differentiation, offering students multiple ways of taking in and expressing information, begins with educators examining four areas: content, process, product, and environment (Tomlinson, 1999). The idea is to find out where students are in the learning process and offer opportunities for forward movement. This is not individualized instruction, nor does it offer an easy way out for the unenthusiastic learner. It affords different learning opportunities that are based on solid curriculum and high expectations. It does allow students to lead with their strengths and their interests in order to understand essential questions and feel successful in the understanding of concepts and skills.

Good teaching calls for realizing that everyone in the classroom is also a teacher. Getting off the stage is not easy for some of us. Our great fear is that our students will not realize the wisdom that we are sure we can impart. True wisdom resides in the ability to step back and facilitate learning.

I begin with three basic premises:

1.   We are all teachers, and we are all learners. My students may be the memory sources for each other. The stories they have to share, the ideas they come up with, or simply the way they put things into words may make all the difference in learning for some of their classmates. According to David Sousa, during every instructional session, the teacher should become the learner and the learner should become the teacher (Sousa, 2002).

2.   Everyone can learn under the right circumstances. We each have our own preferred way of learning, which includes sensory stimulation and memory pathways. Students must be involved in their learning process.

3.   Learning is fun! The brain wants to learn, and, indeed, is learning all the time. When learning is varied and interesting, it is appealing.

With those ideas in mind, let's look at the physical, social/emotional, and cognitive environments in the classroom. Carol Ann Tomlinson (2002) has called these the "root system" in the classroom. It is this system that will set the tone for teaching and learning.

MASLOW'S HIERARCHY OF HUMAN NEEDS

Abraham Maslow (Maslow & Lowery, 1998) is known for his hierarchy of human needs. His theory states that we are motivated to have these needs met. Until and unless these needs are met, humans will continue to focus on satisfying them. His study included successful people like Albert Einstein and Eleanor Roosevelt.

In our search for setting up a classroom in which students feel confident to work and learn together, Maslow's theory can be helpful. We can look at theories and hierarchies that have been postulated by others, like William Glasser (1992) or Stephen Glenn (1990), but I have found that each covers the same basic needs.

Physiological Needs

These are biological needs and must be met first. They consist of needs for oxygen, food, water, and a relatively constant body temperature. These needs are the most important, as an individual deprived of them would focus only on having these met.

Safety Needs

When all physiological needs are satisfied and are no longer controlling thoughts and behaviors, the need for security becomes active. Our

Figure 1.1

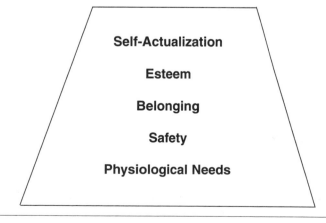

students often show the need for safety and security. In light of recent school shootings and terrorist attacks, this issue must be confronted more directly than ever before.

Need to Belong

When the needs for physiological well-being and for safety are satisfied, the need to belong surfaces. According to Maslow, people seek to overcome feelings of loneliness and isolation. This involves both giving and receiving love and affection and having a sense of belonging.

Esteem

When the first three levels are satisfied, the need for esteem becomes important. This involves needs for both self-esteem and for the regard a person gets from others. Our students require affirmation. They need a secure, firmly based, high level of self-respect, and respect from others. When these needs are satisfied, the student feels self-confident and valuable as a person in the classroom. When these needs are not met, the student may feel helpless and worthless.

Needs for Self-Actualization

After all of the aforementioned needs are satisfied, then the need for self-actualization is set in motion. Self-actualization may be described as a person's need to do what he was born to do.

CLASSROOM ENVIRONMENTS

When I discuss the environment necessary for differentiation, I divide it into three segments: physical environment, social/emotional environment, and cognitive environment. In a sense, they too are hierarchical.

The physical and social/emotional environmental needs overlap somewhat in the hierarchy. Safety and security involve both the physical and the emotional worlds of our students. Belonging and love are part of our social needs; esteem and self-actualization are included in the social/emotional and cognitive environments.

Physical Environment

Beginning with physiological and safety needs, we can address the physical environment of the classroom. We will look a bit beyond the basics cited by Maslow and include areas such as lighting, seating, color,

Figure 1.2

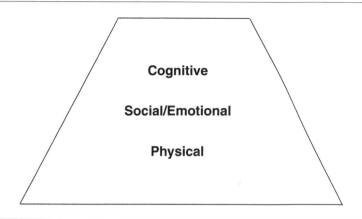

Cognitive

Social/Emotional

Physical

nutrition, music, and humor. Going back to my three premises (Everyone is a teacher, everyone can learn, and learning is fun), we will make our students comfortable and safe. I want my students to walk through the doorway and leave their troubles behind. In some cases, I realize that this is unrealistic, but from experience, I know that this is usually possible.

Tom was a seventh-grade student who had never been allowed to feel that he was smart. He was athletic, nice looking, easy going, and in many ways "all boy." He sometimes got into mischief. Tom was very bright, yet no one considered him so. He had received average to slightly above-average grades.

When Tom came to me, I was the only teacher in our building with any experience with brain-based instruction. My classroom did not resemble any of the other classrooms Tom had been in. The walls had brightly colored posters with positive affirmations on them. In many places in the room, one could find tables or shelves with stuffed animals, coloring books, crayons, art supplies, tape recorders with headsets, and large stacks of paper.

The desks were not in rows, but rather grouped together to form tables. My students almost always sat with a team. They did not necessarily do group work, but no one sat alone. Tom was a little suspicious of all of this. When he sat down, I could tell that he was ready at any moment to move out of that seat.

As Tom discovered that my students were allowed to talk to one another at appropriate times, he slowly started to participate. In fact, for the first time, Tom had the opportunity to learn that he had some leadership desires and skills. His mother told me that he had never been happier. Tom started bringing home papers with "A's" on them. Not just from me. He started getting high grades in every subject. At one point Tom told me that he wasn't sure how he would get through some of his other classes, since the teachers didn't allow him the freedom he needed to interact and learn. I explained to him that his brain needed to adjust to all kinds of learning experiences, and since he knew he would be in our room at various times throughout the day, he could try focusing his attention and learning a bit differently in other rooms. It seemed to work!

An Attractive Environment

Plants, posters, and thought-provoking and pattern-seeking games help a room invite students to come in. Areas that are more casual with bean bag chairs or large pillows present an atmosphere that allows for comfort. Desks that are arranged in small groups or as one large group send the message that "we are all in this together." Although a sense of community can be forged through interaction, setting the stage with a warm atmosphere can make the task easier.

- Decorate your room to make it homier.
- Use posters that have "white space" so you don't overstimulate your students.
- Add plants to the room for a nice touch that adds oxygen as well.
- Let your students bring in some things from home to give them ownership.

Lighting

Many studies have found that both the amount and the type of lighting in a classroom can affect mood and learning. A study of the effects of light on children found that by replacing fluorescent light with a more natural light, attendance increased (Hathaway, Hargreaves, Thompson, & Novitsky, 1992). Another study found that elementary student test scores in three school districts showed significant improvements (20+%) and were strongly correlated with daylight in classrooms (Heschong Mahone Group, 1999).

Mood changes that are affected by the seasons are shown in some studies to be related at least indirectly to the amount of light exposure during the day. These mood changes are sometimes known as Seasonal Affective Disorder. A study revealed that hostility, anger, irritability, and anxiety were higher during the winter months. These symptoms may be related to the temperature, changes in diet and exercise during the winter months, and the amount of daylight or sunlight (Harmatz et al., 2000).

Other more recent studies have found that test scores increase with natural light. We cannot all design our classrooms with large windows for adequate natural light. We may be stuck with fluorescent lights, but it's important to be aware of the need for natural light and to provide it whenever possible.

- Expose students to as much natural light as possible.
- Bring in some lamps with incandescent lighting.
- If you are in a room with few or no windows, make an effort to take your students to an area with natural lighting occasionally.

Temperature

Is it true what they say about "hot-blooded" people? Perhaps. What has been shown in some studies is that higher temperatures change the balance of some of the brain's neurotransmitters. As a result, behavior may also change. Students may become more aggressive in warmer rooms. The ideal temperature according to some research is 68 to 74 degrees Fahrenheit. Balance is what is needed here. Rooms that are too cold cause the brain to make many bodily changes that may also interfere with learning (Jensen & Dabney, 2001).

- Keep your room temperature between 68 and 74 degrees.
- On very warm days, make every effort to find cooler areas in the building and take your students to those areas if possible.
- Give students time to "cool down" after vigorous activities in the gym or on the playground.

Color

The research on the brain's reactions to specific colors has been controversial, if not interesting. There is solid evidence that the brain does respond better to visual input that is colorful. In a study done by psychologists, memory of visual input was enhanced by natural color (Wichmann, Lindsay, Sharpe, & Gegenfurtner, 2002).

Other research suggests that certain colors are more soothing, like pinks and blues. Purple may also soothe, while red may be good for short-term high energy (Howard, 1999). At the very least, it appears that color activates the right hemisphere of the brain. Most of what we do in school is considered left-hemisphere activity; having colorful rooms may assist the brain in using both hemispheres for learning.

- Make your room inviting by using colorful posters and bulletin boards.
- When making posters, use red sparingly. Save it for the important words.
- Use content visuals that are in natural colors.

Nutrition

At each of my workshops, I ask educators if they believe diet affects their students' learning and behavior. The answer is always an overwhelming yes. Although we have little control over what our students eat outside the school, we can influence them greatly. At back-to-school nights and open houses, rather than spend time going over the curriculum that is conveniently written and copied for parents, I spend my time discussing what the parents can do to help in the learning process. This includes providing nutritious food and encouraging adequate sleep.

In each of these areas, we must be good role models. Keep the soda off the desk. Refrain from giving students candy as rewards. There is some research that suggests that sugar will give the brain energy for up to 30 minutes after consumption (Ratey, 2000). After that, however, the students crash from a sugar low and an excess of certain brain chemicals. I always suggest that if you must give candy, give it to them 30 minutes before they leave your classroom!

Breakfast is the most important meal of the day. The brain cannot store energy. Therefore, after a night of fasting, the brain needs energy to run efficiently (Wolfe, Burkman, & Streng, 2000). If you have students that you know do not get breakfast, perhaps your school could provide some nourishment for them. In schools that don't have breakfast programs, keep some nutritious snacks on hand. Fresh fruits and complex carbohydrates are good. Stay away from simple sugars and fats. The Doughnut Days I used to sponsor as Student Council Advisor were probably a bad idea. Doughnuts contain large amounts of sugar and enough fat to keep the blood in the digestive tract instead of in the brain where we need it.

- Check with your students to see who is eating breakfast and what they are eating. Keep a food diary with them for a week so they can see exactly what they are consuming.

- Keep a food pyramid in your classroom. Discuss the importance of the food groups for learning.

- If you have middle or high school students, discuss the body size of advertising models. Let them know how photos are computer generated to make the models look even thinner.

Music

Certainly there are specific tunes that affect your mood. The same is true for our students. Playing music in the classroom can be inspiring, motivating, or calming. It can trigger memory or perhaps make a rainy, dreary day a little less so. When music is playing, students may be more apt to speak in their small groups. It acts as a barrier to embarrassment—others won't be able to hear over the music (Allen, 2002).

Music is also a great way to manage the classroom. Music can signal the end of a session, cleanup time, or a celebration. There are several books available with suggestions for music (Green, 2002; Jensen, 2000a; Sprenger, 2002). Since the brain likes rhythm, this is an easy way to add to the physical environment.

• Have music playing as your students enter your room. Choose music that motivates *you*. If you are motivated, you are more likely to motivate your students.

• If your students want *their* music played, provide break times to do so. Be sure all lyrics are appropriate for school.

• Try playing baroque music during testing. Find baroque selections that are marked "adagio." This provides 40 to 60 beats per minute and is calming. Although some sound-sensitive students may initially object, ask them to give the music a chance. You might try seating them as far from the music as possible.

• Try playing music when the students are working in groups. Let them know that when the music stops, it is time for them to stop talking.

Humor

This specific contribution to the classroom is part of all of the environments. It can do wonders for many situations. Laughter reduces stress while it releases neurotransmitters and tools up the immune system (Society for Neuroscience, 2001). Research has found that understanding and interpreting humor takes separate brain processes. The first is to be receptive to the surprise element. The second is to make sense of the situation. This is exercising part of our memory system called *working memory* (Dye, 1999), which will be discussed fully in Chapter 3. We must also acknowledge that we usually feel good after laughter. This "feel good" part of humor occurs in the emotional center in the brain. We know that anything we learn that has emotion tied to it, we will remember much better. Laugh on!

- Telling jokes or stories that require some thought is good practice for the brain.

- When studying a particular topic, let students find and share jokes about it.

- Joke writing is an art. Perhaps some students would like to write jokes about the content. Be sure they understand that they are not to "put down" the information, but rather add to the learning through the joke.

- Use humor in your presentations. Your students will remember them better.

Water

Our bodies and our brains are largely water (possibly up to 90%, according to Hannaford, 1995). For this reason alone, we must be concerned about hydration. It is very difficult to determine which of our students is hydrated enough. Many of us get most of our water in the foods we eat. Some of us don't like to drink water. But the fact remains that our brains require hydration and, at the very least, we must be cognizant of this fact and patient with our students' needs.

If you are comfortable having water bottles on your students' desks, that is one way of addressing the issue. If water on books and papers is overwhelming to you, how about a drinking fountain or large water cooler in the classroom? If these suggestions are not workable for you in your present situation, have regular drink schedules. Some believe that we should be drinking those eight glasses of water each day. Others suggest that our students should hydrate themselves every 45 minutes or so (Hannaford, 1995).

- Have water available to students in some way: drinking fountain, water bottles, water cooler.

- On particularly warm days, encourage your students to drink water.

- Explain to your students that drinking beverages like soft drinks does not adequately fulfill their need for water. They contain caffeine that depletes the body of water, and sodium, which causes water retention and increases thirst.

Physical Safety

Our students need to be assured that they are safe from physical harm. Recent events have made us all more vigilant in our safety needs. Your school probably has plans for handling possible attacks or intrusions. Assure your students that the school is prepared and there are action plans.

- Review rules and plans for fire, tornado, and other drills in your school's handbook at the start of the year.

- Make and review classroom rules for physical safety.

- Discuss the school's action plans regarding intruders or attacks.

- Assure your students that their safety is of utmost importance to you and the rest of the faculty and staff.

Give your students the opportunity to understand the importance of their physical environment. Assign tasks to keep the room neat and clean. The more involved the students are in the maintenance of their environment, the more aware they will be of the content that is also in the room. This will add to learning retention. In addition, students will feel needed if they have assigned tasks (Glenn, 1990).

Social/Emotional Environment

Maslow's hierarchy addresses safety and security, which include *emotional* safety and security. Belonging and esteem are also dependent on this environment. Basic brain-based teaching principles emphasize the role that emotions play in the learning process. In Daniel Goleman's (1995) groundbreaking book, *Emotional Intelligence,* it is stated that EQ (emotional intelligence) may be more important to success in school and in life than IQ (p. 34).

Goleman (2002) has more recently coauthored a book called *Primal Leadership.* In this text, he has streamlined the basic qualities of emotional intelligence. They are listed as self-awareness, self-management, social awareness, and relationship management.

Self-Awareness

This domain of EQ must really be addressed first. One must be able to identify one's own emotions before being able to deal effectively with others. Many of our students come to school unable to verbalize their emotions. This may be due to the inability of the family to do so, or it may be the lack of access to caring adults to acknowledge and validate the child's feelings. Another aspect of self-awareness is understanding one's strengths and weaknesses. Again, this may take dialogue with others as well as time for reflection.

Figure 1.3

Role Play or Dramatic Review

1. Assign roles: Make sure everyone has a job (actors, time keeper, recorder, reviewer).

2. Set time limits.

3. Student feedback format: Students may write or verbalize feedback (give performers options).

   Follow a format for feedback: praise/suggest/praise

4. Written directions.

5. Role play in small groups for less intimidation.

6. Supply props to assist actors in their performance.

Role Play Discussion Questions or For Pondering

1. What was the outcome? Was one actor happier at the end?

2. What was each character's purpose?

3. What approaches were used?

4. How do you know who was listening? What clues were there for avid listening?

5. Did the characters add information that was not originally included in the scene?

6. Was any important information left out that would have made a difference in the final outcome?

SOURCE: Adapted from *Creative Training Techniques*, Bob Pike Group

A self-aware student will be able to do several things. Most important, she will be able to recognize and name her own emotions. This may take practice and some helpful activities such as the following:

• Use the book, *My Many Colored Days*, by Dr. Seuss. Read the book to your students and discuss the emotions related to color. At various times, ask your students what color day they are having. Give them the opportunity to share with partners or small groups about their day, or give them time to write in journals about their feelings and the causes of those feelings.

• As you take attendance, ask your students to also give you a barometer of how they feel. Use a scale from 1 to 10, with 10 being "feeling great" and 1, "I wish I were in a hole." You could also go back to the Seuss book and have them say a color along with declaring they are present.

• Role play situations that involve feelings. Follow the *role play suggestions* in Figure 1.3.

Figure 1.4

Self-Awareness Survey

1. Today I feel

   _____

2. The last time I felt this way was

   _____

3. The reason for this feeling back then was

   _____

4. I feel this way today because

   _____

5. When I feel this way I want to

   a. Talk about it with others

   b. Be alone

   c. Do something interesting to get my mind off it

   d. Write about it in my journal

• Use the ever-popular posters of facial expressions to discuss and mimic how those expressions let others know about feelings.

• Model self-awareness. Let your students know when you are experiencing a strong emotion that they may be able to relate to. Take a few minutes to let them share or write about a time they felt the same way.

• Use self-awareness questions or checklists to give students the opportunity to reflect on their current feelings. (See Figure 1.4.)

• Have an emotional word wall. When students are emotional and are having difficulty verbalizing their feelings, ask them to pick out an

Figure 1.5

<table>
<tr><td colspan="2" align="center">**Feelings Wall**</td></tr>
<tr><td>Today I feel . . .</td><td>Right now I feel . . .</td></tr>
<tr><td>Happy</td><td>Anxious</td></tr>
<tr><td>Sad</td><td>Scared</td></tr>
<tr><td>Excited</td><td>Mad</td></tr>
<tr><td>Angry</td><td>Nervous</td></tr>
<tr><td>Bored</td><td>Silly</td></tr>
<tr><td>Baffled</td><td>Embarrassed</td></tr>
<tr><td>Concerned</td><td>Excited</td></tr>
<tr><td>Curious</td><td>Proud</td></tr>
</table>

emotion word. Add words as new emotions are mentioned. (In one class, students competed in finding new words to define their feelings. For instance, Genna walked in with a big smile and said, "Today, I am elated!" We added the word, she defined it, and others began looking for feeling words that would be new. It was a great way to increase their vocabulary.) (See Figure 1.5.)

Self-Management

Once a student is aware and can reflect on her feelings, she can begin to manage her moods and actions. Most often, when we are feeling positive emotions, our behavior is positive. When negative emotions take over, a process that Goleman (1995) refers to as "emotional hijacking," the results can be quite disturbing.

This is especially important in light of the suggestion that emotions are contagious (Goleman, 1995). In our classrooms, this suggests that our positive attitudes and emotions can motivate others. Negative emotions must be controlled to prevent the spread of anger, fear, or hostility. A student with self-management skills can control anger and frustration, is better at handling stress, and has less social anxiety.

Self-management also includes self-motivation. If a student can control impulsive behavior by dealing with emotions, he can also use emotion to motivate himself. If the physical and emotional environments are conducive to feeling and expressing emotions appropriately, students will be less inclined to give up when things aren't going exactly the way they had hoped.

To promote self-management:

• Teach your students basic coping skills. These may include exercise, meditation, self-talk, adequate sleep, and proper nutrition.

• Using a reference like Martin Seligman's (1985) *The Optimistic Child,* discuss the importance of optimism.

• Provide time to journal and emphasize the importance of writing about feelings and experiences. Recent research suggests that when we write about our experiences, we feel that we have more control over them. (Restak, 2000).

• Provide a recipe for your students to follow when their emotions seem to be taking over. This must be attempted before the situation has gotten out of hand. A sample recipe may include the following:

1. Take a deep breath.

2. Count to ten.

3. Ask yourself or your partner intelligent questions about the situation and listen carefully.

4. Consider what others might do in the situation.

5. Formulate a plan and try it.

• Model good self-management skills. When you share your emotions with your students, be sure to explain how you are dealing with them.

• Think aloud. As you are thinking through tasks and processes in the classroom, verbalize the thought process you are following. This gives students the opportunity to hear and understand how you are managing yourself during different tasks.

Social Awareness

One of the most important components of social awareness is empathy. The ability to understand how someone else feels is vital to strong communication. In just milliseconds, our brains consider the emotional overtones in every conversation. Facial expression, body language, and tone all send messages to the individual who is empathic. From these messages, responses are gleaned that can contribute to a worthwhile and productive conversation. This is vital to a productive classroom that honors diversity.

Our students are very aware of the social strata that have evolved in their school, their neighborhood, and their classroom. It is imperative that we, as good educators, also be aware of the social hierarchy, as it will affect the dynamics in the classroom. In the book *Cliques* by Charlene Giannetti and Margaret Sagarese (2001), the general social divisions of middle school are defined. I have taken their information and shared it among thousands of elementary and secondary teachers in my workshops. They agree that (a) cliques begin in the primary grades, and (b) these statistics appear to be accurate for secondary schools as well.

According to *Cliques* (pp. 20–21), our students fall into four categories:

Popular. About 35% of students are in the popular crowd. This is the "in" group—the athletic kids, affluent kids, and the pretty kids. These kids are the trendsetters. They've been social creatures before most kids their age socialized. They look like they're in control and having fun. But are they?

Drawback to being "popular": You never know how long that popularity is going to last.

Fringe. About 10% of the population fall into this category. The fringe group sometimes hangs around with the popular group, but only when invited. This group doesn't know from day to day where they belong. They dress like the popular group and try to act like them as well. For whatever reason, it is enough for them to be at the beck and call of the populars. They want to be in control and have fun. But can they?

Friendship Circles. This group comprises about 45% of the population. It consists of small groups of friends. They know they are not popular, but they don't care. They have the friendship and loyalty that they need. These groups are not all alike. Some may be labeled geeks or nerds. Others may be considered greasers or bangers. But the fact remains that although they may feel somewhat hostile toward the popular group, they have their niche and seem to be content.

Loners. This last group consists of about 10% of the population. These kids have no friends. There are varied reasons for this. Some of these kids are very bright, creative, and in a class of their own. Some have very little emotional intelligence and use inappropriate behaviors, such as invading personal space, that make others want to stay away from them. Some of them even we teachers dread being around. Many of them wish to be in a group, but have simply never been accepted. These kids could grow up to be influential and successful, or they could become school shooters. Many of these kids are unhappy.

Empathy becomes a major factor in the classroom when we have such diverse and obvious social groups. Often in the classroom, our students "put up with" each other when we place them in groups. But we have all heard moans and groans when our students are asked to pair and share and they are displeased with their partner. Empathy must be modeled and taught.

• When speaking to the class or to a student, verbalize the emotion you are feeling and ask your student(s) if or when they have had that same emotion. Discuss it or write about it.

• In the content areas such as social studies or science, try to get students to put themselves in the shoes of the people in history, or those in a geographical area you are studying, or even in the shoes of an inventor or scientist. How did they feel? How would you feel?

• Read stories or dialogues and ask students to listen carefully to try to understand how the character feels.

• Have students bring in cartoon strips, read them to the class, and describe how the characters are feeling.

Relationship Management

This final area of emotional intelligence is the key to providing an emotional environment that is conducive to learning for the diverse groups that we are seeing today. The sequence of recognizing one's emotions, handling one's emotions, recognizing emotions in others, and finally, handling other's emotions may appear to be challenging. Yet many of our students do come to us with some, if not all, of these skills operating.

If our students are adept at relationship management, the emotional environment will be one that is stable and comfortable. There will be fewer conflicts, and those that arise will be dealt with more easily. Students will be more democratic in their dealings with those from different social groups. In general, the student population will be friendlier, and those that are very facile in this area will be sought out by their peers. Perhaps some of those social groups will change or even merge as the overall emotional intelligence of the group improves.

Cooperative learning groups and teams are vital to the development of EQ. Learning is social; therefore, for our students to really learn well, these social skills must be taught. Just as manners must be taught, rapport skills and group skills must also be taught.

- Role play situations that demonstrate how various group circumstances might be handled.

- When assigning group work, have mock group meetings to demonstrate how to handle the material and respect each participant.

- Begin with small groups, perhaps even dyads or triads, to give students practice in working with others.

- Utilize short problem-solving sessions with diverse problems to allow the interests and expertise of different group members to emerge.

- Set up situations where students will need to compromise.

- Teach both listening skills and questioning skills.

- Include in your class rules that there is no teasing or humiliation allowed in your classroom.

The social/emotional environment can easily make the difference between a class that is easy to handle and where learning takes place quickly, and a class that makes every day difficult.

Cognitive Environment

Once the physical and emotional environments are set, it is time to examine the cognitive environment. It is through this environment that we work on esteem and self-actualization. What do we need for our students to learn and remember? Since all brains learn differently, are there any commonalities I can work on to help my whole class? Thankfully, the answer is yes. There are some brain basics that will affect all students to varying degrees. The characteristics of a strong cognitive environment include predictability, feedback, novelty, choice, challenge, and reflection.

Predictability

If we want the brain to learn, we must reduce stress. Small amounts of stress may be helpful in learning, but in general, stress causes the brain to initiate the stress response, which interferes with learning. Especially at

Figure 1.6   Cognitive environments provide ritual, novelty, feedback, challenge, choice, and reflection. Various areas of the brain respond to these elements, which allow brains to make new connections and reach higher level thinking.

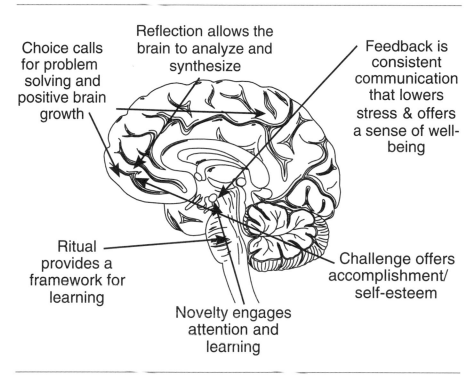

Choice calls for problem solving and positive brain growth

Reflection allows the brain to analyze and synthesize

Feedback is consistent communication that lowers stress & offers a sense of well-being

Ritual provides a framework for learning

Challenge offers accomplishment/ self-esteem

Novelty engages attention and learning

stressful times, the brain seeks predictability (Jensen, 1998). Have you ever come home from a taxing day at school and vegged out in front of the television? Most television programs are extremely predictable. This allows our brains to work at a minimum while feeling confident of knowing what will happen next.

School and classroom situations can be very unpredictable, even for us. I may expect that my students will be on time. I may expect that my lesson will be received well. I may expect that my principal will like my plans for next week. But I cannot count on my predictions. These situations are not in my control; however, there are ways to help our students feel in control through predictable situations. Our students expect predictability from us. This may come in the form of returning papers on time. It may be in expecting consistency in following classroom rules and consequences of breaking those rules. They may look forward to a predictable event like a celebration when they do well.

Rituals are predictable events. Music playing as the students enter may start off the predictable events of the day. Your greeting may be a ritual that puts the brain at ease. There are many predictable events in your classroom of which you may not even be aware. Here are some tips for using rituals in your classroom:

- Set up rituals early in the year. Have several established on the first day.

- Use rules as part of your rituals. Have them posted and refer to them when necessary.

- Preview material. The preview provides the brain with some information that it can expect. Then when you begin the new material, it doesn't seem so new. The students have some small connections to it.

- Keep your promises. How many times have I heard, "But you said you'd give us our papers back today!"

Feedback

There is much research to back up the need for continuous feedback. Neuroscientist William Greenough believes that interactive feedback is required in order to learn from experience. Educational researchers Marzano, Pickering, and Pollack (2001a) have analyzed data supporting the effectiveness of feedback. According to their book, *Classroom Instruction That Works,* the most beneficial feedback involves explanations pertaining to the accuracies or inaccuracies of student work. Based on the thorough research in this area, suggestions for offering feedback to your students might include the following:

- Provide feedback in a timely manner. Immediate feedback is beneficial as long as there are not others around to make the student feel inadequate. Sometimes we must wait for opportune times. Giving papers back weeks late may be ineffective as students may have forgotten some of the material or lost their motivation for learning it.

- Be specific with feedback. In my earlier years of teaching, I would find myself writing simple phrases on essays that were well-written like, "Nice job!" This feedback did not help those students grow in their writing.

- Let students choose the type of feedback they would like to receive. When students are assessing each other, give them the choice as to whether the feedback they give is oral or written.

- Give students the opportunity to provide their own feedback. If students have a stake in their learning, self-assessment is very valuable. They can keep track of their scores, video or audiotape themselves and critique these tapes, or use their journals for feedback.

• When students work in groups or on teams, their teammates can provide feedback. You are only one person. It is desirable that students interact and receive feedback continuously. Teach your teams how to give effective feedback. Use the same strategy that is used in role play: praise, suggest, and praise again.

• Keep in mind that quality is important. The quality of the feedback is directly dependent on the quality of the observation. Your students may need some skill work in observing. Create checklists with your students' input to provide greater understanding of the process.

Novelty

The brain responds well to novelty. As long as predictability exists in the classroom, students will be able to handle some novelty. Something that is unique to the learning situation will garner attention because our brains have been programmed to respond to unusual stimuli—a survival skill we learned hundreds of years ago when we needed to be aware of danger. But for the classroom, a little novelty is good; too much novelty can cause stress.

• Using novelty requires new and different approaches to learning. If a novel situation gets a positive response from your students, don't repeat it for awhile. The brain tends to habituate to stimuli. In other words, after repetition, it won't be novel anymore.

• Costumes and accessories, such as hats, scarves, and flags, add novelty to learning.

• Field explorations (like field trips, but with some interaction) add novelty to learning.

• Music that represents the theme of what you are teaching can provide novelty.

• On those rainy or dreary days when you know your students are dragging and not very interested in learning, provide novelty through background music, a change in lighting (probably brighter, but dimmer might work), or a change in location (maybe a trip to the library or gym, or switch rooms with another teacher for the day or class period).

Choice

Some researchers have found that the brain responds positively to choice. Both the prefrontal cortex (responsible for decision making, future planning, and critical thinking) and the amygdala (emotional area) respond in a positive manner (Bechara, Damasio, H., Damasio, A., & Lee, 1999).

Offering students choices can increase motivation. Think about this: Instead of always doling out an assignment, what about offering some options that might pique their curiosity? "You may do the problems on page 56, or you may come to my desk and pick up a packet of material and follow the directions inside."

- Giving younger students simple options may be best.

- Choice can be used particularly well in assessment. Keeping different learning styles and memory preferences in mind, offer students various projects and products to choose from.

- Perhaps students could even choose what content they want to cover. Of course, they can't redesign the curriculum, but they may feel more involved if they get to choose what to cover first.

- I redesigned the effective KWL chart. This is a chart to fill out with, first, what they Know. Then what they Want to know. And finally, what they have Learned. It is used by many teachers of both adults and children. I added two more letters. Mine is KWHLU. The K, W, and L are the same. H stands for How do you want to learn it? The U is for how will you Use it in your world? (See Figure 1.7.)

Challenge

William Greenough (Blum, 1999) feels that the other ingredient to learning from experience besides feedback is challenge. Differentiation is a strong component here. What is challenging to one student may cause absolute fear in another.

I like Lev Vygotsky's (1980) approach to challenge. He believed that if we offer tasks that are a bit beyond the learner's reach, we should provide support along the way. In other words, the learner requires a coach. This can be the teacher or a peer. We often give students challenges and provide nothing more than a textbook. A textbook may or may not be an adequate coach.

- Provide challenges for your students, keeping in mind different learning styles and readiness levels.

- Provide coaching for each challenge. Some students will require more coaching than others.

Figure 1.7

K What do we *know?*	W What do we *want* to know?	H *How* do we want to learn it?	L What have we *learned?*	U How will we *use* this formation in our world?

- Be sure that you assign relevant projects that are challenging. Even our brightest students will resent difficult or challenging projects that are not associated with current goals and standards.

- To some of our students, everything is challenging. Keep that in mind and provide coaching for them, too.

Reflection

Silence and reflection can enhance learning (Kessler, 2000). It is at this quiet time that students have the opportunity to reflect on their emotions about what is happening. And reflecting upon the content allows for higher-level thinking such as synthesizing the material to make the proper connections in the brain. Reflection will also help memory. To put it simply, reflection is a repetition of what one has learned. It is the processing of the experience and re-evaluation of perceptions. This is the basis of new knowledge (Boud & Walker, 1991).

- Although many teachers feel that there is little time for reflection, keep in mind that it is necessary for understanding and retention.

- Use journal writing for reflection on learning.

- All must respect quiet time in the classroom. Reflection time or "down time" is not a waste of time. When material is new or difficult, reflection time becomes even more important.

- When the opportunity presents itself, do some sharing after reflection time. Students can share in small groups or with partners. They may find another student's synthesis of the material helpful.

THE STAGE IS SET

A classroom that is conducive and sensitive to the differences in our students comes about not through recipes, but through a thinking pattern. As educators, we always need to be thinking about what might work with our students. Assessment is an ongoing process that we utilize to help our students learn. Creating an environment that addresses the physical, emotional, and cognitive needs of students provides the background for differentiation.

DIFFERENT STROKES

 1. A teacher who attended one of my summer workshops shared an interesting way to differentiate using the cognitive environment characteristics. For her eighth-grade mythology class she set up the following learning and research centers. Each had Internet access.

Predictability Center: This center was for her students who seemed stressed. Their assignment was to create a family tree and time line for the mythology characters.

Choice Center: These students were able to choose a mythological creature that had not been previously studied. A poster, interview, or news article could be written.

Novelty Center: Using any preferred medium (e.g., clay, papier-mâché), these students were to create a scene from a myth not yet covered.

Challenge Center: The students were to create a PowerPoint presentation comparing Hercules with a modern hero who was not Michael Jordan! The characteristics, goals, and accomplishments had to be compared and contrasted.

Reflection Center: This assignment was an essay sharing the effects mythology has on present day society.

2. Using teams can be one of the strongest components in a classroom. For differentiation purposes, multiple teams are helpful. You may want a base team, writing team, problem-solving team, question-generating team, or study team. This gives students the opportunity to work on social skills and work at different readiness and interest levels.

Learning Strengths 2

"I never realized how important different learning environments are. Just understanding that has made a big difference in my classroom. But I know that there is more to it," Janice says as we sit at the lunch table.

"Sit with your students at lunch once in awhile," I offer. "You can learn a lot about them in the cafeteria. See who is sitting with whom. The social hierarchy will really present itself there."

"Margo, I saw your students sitting and working at different activities. What was that about? Don't you worry about what is going on when you can't watch them all at once? I'm so afraid of losing control!" Janice declares.

"If you have them working on something interesting, working together, you've hit their readiness or interest levels, then it's not much of a problem," Margo replies. "What you saw were some learning centers that were designed for different learning strengths."

"What kind of learning strengths?"

"Did you ever talk about learning styles or modalities in college?" I ask.

"In one of the classes we talked about that a little bit."

"Well, learning strengths develop as the brain learns. Many of us tend to have a preference for one or more of our senses. I prefer visual information. My friend, Glenn, remembers very little that he reads, but he remembers everything he hears."

Janice looks perplexed, "I thought this was really old stuff. Straight out of the fifties or sixties."

Margo and I look at each other. "Watch out what you call old stuff!" Margo quips. "Marilee and I are 'old stuff' and you're asking us for help. This information has been around a while, and recent research is supporting its importance."

I smile. "Janice, this really changed my teaching and made my life easier. Whenever the students are learning and they're happy, the classroom is a great place to be."

We begin to fill Janice in on what we are referring to. It doesn't take long to understand some of the differences that would be found among students in every classroom. Margo shares the following story with her.

It is the first day of school. Jeffrey and Elise are both excited about the new school year. At Jeffrey's house, the alarm goes off earlier than usual and he takes great care in dressing, as he wants to look a little extra special for this first day. Jeffrey takes some time in the bathroom fixing his hair. He is eager to see his friends and check out the new students. He has heard that several new girls have entered the district and some will be in his class.

Elise's mom wakes her before she leaves for work. Elise has a brand new outfit and she is excited about seeing what the other girls will be wearing.

Jeffrey checks over the contents of his book bag before he leaves. Everything appears to be in order: Number 2 pencils, three folders, notebook paper, black ink pens, a compass, and a protractor. He zips up the bag and zips out the door.

Elise takes a last-minute look at her hair. "Perfect," she thinks as she looks around for her school supplies. Did she remember to pack those supplies that Mom bought? Oh yes, there's paper, pens, and pencils. That ought to do it until the teachers tell her exactly what they expect. She heads for the bus.

The students mill around in the school yard until the bell rings at 7:45. They then enter the building and head to their homerooms. Jeffrey and Elise are in the same room this year. They've been in school together since first grade. They smile and nod to each other as they head for their seats. Jeffrey sits in the front while Elise heads to the back corner where she talks to some of her friends.

Mrs. Warmth enters the room. She has been in the hall greeting students. Elise really likes this teacher. She smiles a lot, listens carefully to the kids, and always shares interesting experiences.

Jeffrey wishes he had Mr. Stuff for homeroom. That is one interesting teacher. He has all kinds of things in the room to look at. Mr. Stuff teaches science, and although Jeffrey will have him for one class period later in the day, he would love to be in his homeroom as well.

After Mrs. Warmth takes attendance and lunch count, the bell rings for first period. Jeffrey, Elise, and the rest of the students gather their belongings and head for Miss Rigid's language arts class. "All right, boys and girls, you will be sitting alphabetically, so don't get too comfortable." Jeffrey smiles at this. He's in the first part of the alphabet, so he's certain to have a seat up front. He doesn't want to miss anything! Besides, one of the new girls' last names is Adams. He wouldn't mind sitting by her.

Elise rolls her eyes as her name is called. She's sitting in the second row, second seat. All of her friends are in the back of the room. *Why can't I change my last name?* she complains to herself as she settles in the new seat.

The textbooks are on the desks. Jeffrey carefully puts his name in his book and looks through the table of contents as Miss Rigid suggests. Elise opens her book, writes her name, and quickly closes it. *Another year of boring textbooks,* she thinks as she turns around to wave to Cheryl.

"Elise!" shouts Miss Rigid. "It's the first day of school; let's not start breaking the rules yet!"

Elise rolls her eyes and turns back around. She figures she'll give this woman ten minutes. If things don't get active, it will be time to daydream the class period away. There is no way she can sit for 45 minutes listening to a lecture and staring at a book.

Jeffrey sits up eagerly waiting for new information and an assignment. He has his new pen and paper ready.

DIFFERENT LEARNERS/DIFFERENT TEACHERS

Both of these students are eager to start the new year. They want to go to school. Why does Jeffrey eagerly await new information and Elise prepare to daydream her way through class? Does she not care about learning?

The first period bell rings and Elise jumps! She was thinking about the football game on Friday night. She throws her book and supplies into her bag and lines up at the door with the other students. Jeffrey finishes writing down the assignment and joins her at the door.

"Do we have homework?" Elise asks him.

Jeffrey looks at her and wonders how she got this far. "Call me after school and I'll give you the assignment," he says with a sigh.

They enter Mrs. Precise's math class. The desks that were in the room last year are gone. They have been replaced with modular tables. "Sit wherever you want," Mrs. Precise announces. "We'll be working in groups this year. I've chosen your groups for this first unit. After that, we'll create some special interest groups."

Elise smiles at the possibilities in this classroom. No daydreaming here. From the feel of this setup, she can learn a lot this year in math.

Mrs. Precise interrupts Elise's thoughts. "Okay, the first thing we will do is go to the board. I want to see you work some problems in pairs."

Elise jumps up with glee, grabs Cheryl, and picks a spot right in front of her teacher. She is eager to show off her math ability. Jeffrey slowly rises, nods to one of his friends and goes to the board with him. He can't wait till this part of the class is over; he'd rather stay at his desk to work. He is also concerned about this group work; he hopes he won't end up doing everyone else's work.

What a difference a class period can make for some students! It is now obvious that both Jeffrey and Elise care about learning. They just learn differently. It is up to their school and its teachers to provide learning opportunities that fit.

DIFFERENTIATION THROUGH SENSORY PATHWAYS

From the short observation of Jeffrey, it looks as though he is a visual learner. He likes to sit up front, and he enjoys looking at his books. He is also an independent learner. It is uncomfortable for him to work in groups. He is successful at the "school game." He knows how to take in semantic information and probably is very good at giving it back on both teacher-made assessments and standardized tests.

Elise, on the other hand, needs to move and talk. She is a kinesthetic learner. By working in pairs or groups, Elise has the opportunity to move and to process information through kinesthetic and auditory channels. Auditory learners need to talk as much as they need to listen. That is how learning becomes real to them.

Behavioral psychologist Andrew Meltzoff recommends that teachers use various ways of inputting information (Meltzoff, 2000). All information enters our brains through our senses. There are not only preferred sensory systems of which educators must be made aware, but it makes perfect "sense" that the more senses that are activated, the more likely information will be encoded. In other words, Elise can take in information visually if she is allowed to move and talk as well. It is understood that we are all capable of using all of our sensory pathways (unless there is a physical problem). Some students are simply more balanced than others in their ability to take in information in different ways.

In my classrooms, I find that if I think VAK (visual, auditory, kinesthetic) for every lesson, students not only learn more quickly and easily, they enjoy it. If we want our students to care about learning, they must feel successful in the process.

Mrs. Precise has the concept. She begins her lesson for the kinesthetic learner. First, the students are at the board. The opportunity for large-muscle movement is provided. The students are working in pairs. This provides the auditory learner with input and the opportunity for output. It also helps reduce stress. Those visual learners will soon "see" all kinds of information on that board. But even better, this is the way this teacher accesses prior knowledge—a key to learning. Since the brain is a meaning-making organ, making connections with previous learning through different modalities allows each student to make sense of the learning. Once Mrs. Precise has ascertained what her students already know, she can use those hooks for future learning.

WHY SENSORY PATHWAYS?

Sensory information is sent from our nervous system to the brain stem. From the brain stem it goes to the central filtering station in the middle of the brain called the thalamus. The thalamus sends this information to its designated area of the neocortex. The neocortex is where higher-level thinking takes place. Each sense has a place called an association cortex. For instance, auditory information is sent via the thalamus to the auditory association cortex. The information is examined, and if it is important and should be attended to, another brain structure becomes involved—the

Figure 2.1

Information Processing

1. Information enters the brain through the senses. All sensory information except the sense of smell is processed the same way.

2. It goes through the brain stem to the limbic structure called the thalamus.

3. The thalamus sorts the information and sends it to the various areas in the neocortex.

4. Visual information goes to the visual cortex in the occipital lobe. Auditory information goes to the auditory cortex in the temporal lobe. Kinesthetic information goes to the motor strip and the cerebellum.

5. If the information requires immediate attention, the reticular activating system in the brain stem releases chemical messages to focus attention.

6. If the information is important and factual, the limbic structure called the hippocampus catalogs it for long-term memory. If the information is important and emotional, the limbic structure called the amygdala catalogs it for long-term memory.

7. The information is then stored in the various areas of the neocortex.

reticular activating system, which is found in the brain stem. This powerful structure can send messages throughout the brain. It "wakes up" the brain to the identified information (Kittredge, 1990).

All of your senses are always "on." You are bombarded with sensory information every second. It would be impossible to pay attention to all of it. And you wouldn't want to. For instance, until you read the next few words, you are probably not aware of how your chair feels on your bottom. Or how your toes feel in your shoes. This is not important information unless you are extremely uncomfortable in one of these areas. Your brain helps you focus on what is important.

Since all information is received through our five senses, many researchers feel that a preference is developed for a specific sense (Dunn & Dunn, 1987; Grinder, 1991; Markova, 1992; Sprenger, 2002). Just as most of us develop a preference for using one hand or the other, and that one becomes "dominant," many people likewise appear to have dominant sensory pathways. Through their experiences, genetics, and their brain development, one of the senses has come to operate better for them than the others. We can designate this sense or modality as their *learning strength*. Since 1971, I have been working with both adults and children and have found that individuals will always learn best if they begin with that strength.

The importance of understanding these sensory approaches to learning will become clearer when we examine how memory works and look at memory problems. According to Barbe and Swassing, sensation, perception, and memory together create a modality (Guild & Garger, 1998). You see, you have a visual, auditory, and kinesthetic memory system. What about the other two senses? Do they have memories? Clearly, we have all been taken back in time by certain smells or tastes. These are usually lumped in with the kinesthetic sense since they involve an action (Markova & Powell, 1998).

Michael Grinder (1991), author of *Righting the Educational Conveyor Belt*, examines a classroom of 30 students. He says that approximately 22 of these students are very balanced in their ability to retrieve and retain information through all of the sensory pathways. Of the 8 remaining, 2 or 3 are having a difficult time learning because of problems outside the classroom. Then there are 5 or 6 students who have a very difficult time with any sensory pathway other than their strength. He calls these students "translators," as they must translate information from the other senses into their preferred style. Translation is difficult at best for many of them. And much can be lost in the translation. These are the students who need more help. We may recognize them as the students whose hands are usually raised for questions or who march up to our desks for help immediately following a lesson.

CHARACTERISTICS OF SENSORY PATHWAYS

Certain characteristics have been identified that can be attributed to sensory preferences. Some of these may be familiar to you. However, if it's been awhile, take another look. I think you'll be surprised at what you might have forgotten or what has been more recently discovered. Typically, when observing the visual, auditory/verbal, and tactile/kinesthetic learners, some of the following behaviors may be observed:

Visual

- Rolls eyes
- Follows you around the room with his or her eyes
- Is distracted by movement
- Loves handouts, work on the board, overheads, and any visual presentations
- Often speaks rapidly
- Will usually retrieve information by looking up and to the left
- Says things like, "I see what you mean," or "I get the picture"

Auditory/Verbal

- May answer rhetorical questions
- Talks a lot; may talk to self
- Distracted by sound
- Enjoys cassette tape work and listening to you speak
- Likes to have material read aloud
- Usually speaks distinctly
- Will usually retrieve information by looking from side to side while listening to his or her internal tape recorder
- Says things like, "Sounds good to me," or "I hear what you're saying"

Kinesthetic/Tactile

- Sits very comfortably or casually; usually slouched or lots of fidgeting ; leans back in chair, taps pencil
- Often speaks very slowly, feeling each word
- Distracted by comfort variations, such as temperature, light

- Needs hands-on experiences
- Distracted by movement—often his or her own
- Will usually retrieve information by looking down to access the same feelings or movements that were involved in receiving the information
- Says things like, "I need a concrete example" or "That feels right"

SENSORY SYSTEMS

We've come so far with brain research, and we still don't have all the answers. Fortunately, more information is available now that deals with how our sensory systems operate. It is this information that can help us understand some of the differences we see in our students.

Let's look briefly at information processing. As I stated earlier, information enters our brains through our senses. Each sense has a passageway. The thalamus sorts information and sends it to the top layer of the brain, the neocortex. The neocortex has an area for each type of sensory stimuli. The visual cortex processes visual information, the auditory cortex processes sounds, and the somatic cortex processes touch. The information from each is then sent to the rhinal cortex. Here the senses are put back together into one representation. From the rhinal cortex, the information is sent to the hippocampus. This important memory structure receives information from several convergence zones in the brain. It is here that the information can change from a simple perception of what is happening to an abstract concept (LeDoux, 2002). (See Figure 2.2.)

With this information, we can see how vital our sensory systems are to learning. The concept of having a preferred sensory system has been conveyed by educators and researchers (DePorter, 2000; Grinder 1991; Markova, 1992; Rose & Nicholl, 1997). When I first learned this information, I thought it was vital that I know the preferred sensory passageway of each of my students. This is interesting information for a teacher to have, and it is very helpful if students have some difficulties learning. But it is more important that the students understand their preferences, so they can lead with their strengths.

VISUAL MEMORY PREFERENCE

The learner who has this preference prefers to see information. It sounds simplistic, but there are in fact at least two types of visual learners. Some are able to easily see and understand graphs and charts, while others are simply print-oriented (Kline, 1997). I am a print-oriented visual learner. I

Figure 2.2

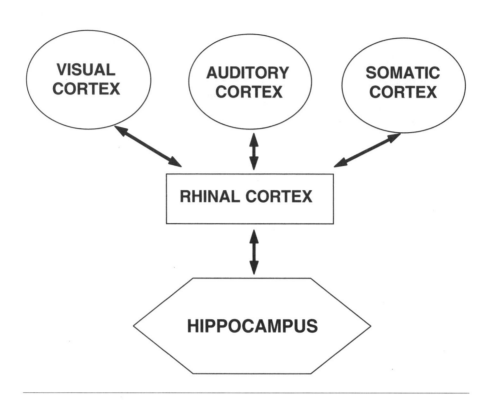

often disappoint others because I don't recall the color of their carpet or their new kitchen. I do, however, remember the printed word. When asked a question, if I have read the information, I picture the words, then the page, and finally I can close the book in my mind and state the title. You can generally tell a visual learner by the eye contact she will give you. These learners may have some of the characteristics described earlier. They may be happy as clams just to have you say, "Open your books to page 54 and look at . . ." Learning is real to them if they can see it. Many of these learners have good visualization skills. So, if they have participated in a kinesthetic activity that involved learning a concept, they can conjure up that episode in their mind's eye in order to recall it. Some with this preference will have strong spatial skills and will be able to visualize shapes and sizes with little difficulty. Because they often can easily visualize words or problems, spelling and math may be undemanding for them. Some of these students are very neat as they are so aware of how things look. Untidiness can be a source of stress for them. Movies, field trips, maps, graphs, charts, and pictures will usually pique their interest.

Print-oriented learners can become bogged down in the printed word. Most of them are able to learn from the same experiences as other visual learners. They may, however, need to be prodded to do so. For instance, reading a graph is quite different from reading a printed page. Encouragement and assistance may be necessary for the task. This preference also includes writing. Writing information gives visual learners the opportunity to see how concepts fit together. They may take copious notes, even if they won't need to look at them a second time.

AUDITORY/VERBAL MEMORY PREFERENCE

The auditory preference usually involves both hearing and speaking. Our auditory areas and speech areas in the brain are in close proximity. Typically these learners enjoy listening to others as well as listening to themselves talk! Often these students have strong language skills. Their vocabularies are frequently extensive. They enjoy words and speak in a rhythmical fashion. Some of these individuals pick up foreign languages and dialects easily (Markova, 1992). These students may have musical talents. Tone, pitch, rhythm, and rhyme may be appealing to them. At the same time, these students may be sound sensitive. In other words, certain noises may be annoying to them. As they are learning or concentrating, extraneous noises, such as the radiator, may cause them to lose concentration. These are the students who say, "Tell him to stop clicking his pen," or "She's got to stop coughing—it's driving me crazy. I can't think!" I had one student tell me, "He's breathing too loud!" Spelling is usually done by sounding words out. Perhaps this is why they don't like to write much. Their spelling is often wrong—after all, you can't even spell *phonetically*, phonetically!

Many educators believe that those with auditory preferences can listen all day long. That is simply not true. What makes learning real to these students is being able to talk about it. Group work has saved many auditory processors. Working on group or team projects gives these students the opportunity to talk through the material.

KINESTHETIC/TACTILE MEMORY PREFERENCES

The kinesthetic/tactile preference includes different types of learners. We often think of these students as simply wigglers and jigglers. My own daughter falls into this category. School was not a happy place for her most of the time. In particular, her teachers with a visual preference found Marnie's movement a distraction. However, this is not the only characteristic of a child or adult who follows this preference.

Hands-On Learners

The hands-on, tactile-kinesthetic learners need to "do" something in order to learn it. They usually process best through assembling, taking things apart, working with textured materials, and manipulating objects. Math manipulatives have really made a difference in the lives of these learners. My husband, Scott, is a hands-on learner. He doesn't read the VCR manual (or any other directions); he plays with the controls until he figures it out.

Whole-Body Learners

The whole-body, tactile-kinesthetic learners need to become what they are learning. This may include role playing, exercising, building, giving live demonstrations, and using whole-body movements.

Doodlers

The doodling tactile-kinesthetic learners learn through drawing, coloring, and doodling. Being able to do this at their desks while discussion is going on actually may help them listen. With this learner, I have to remind myself that the doodling is "turning on his brain."

Many of these students have good fine and large motor skills. They may be very coordinated and do well in sports. These students are often mislabeled as hyperactive since sitting still is a major problem for some of them. Often if the teacher stays in close proximity to a mover and shaker, it will keep him calmer. An affirming touch to the shoulder may also calm him.

PERCEPTUAL PATTERNS

Dr. Dawna Markova has written several books on the subject of the way we learn. She compares our minds to an orchestra. We are like different instruments: They are played differently. They sound different. But together they make beautiful music. The trick is to know what instrument you have and how to play it. For many years, I was a teacher playing the trombone. Teaching the trombone to a whole class of students—with very few actually having a trombone! Markova approaches sensory preferences from another perspective. Since we all have five senses, and use all five senses, she categorizes learners into six different patterns:

When we look at the whole child, there are times when understanding these perceptual patterns is helpful. There are some differences in

Figure 2.3

Pattern	Preference	Characteristics
Visual-Auditory-Kinesthetic	1. Seeing & Showing 2. Hearing & Saying 3. Experiencing & Doing	Read and tell stories; good eye contact; can sit still for long periods; shies away from sports
Visual-Kinesthetic-Auditory	1. Seeing & Showing 2. Experiencing & Doing 3. Hearing & Saying	Good eye contact; neat; speaks with hands; shies away from public speaking
Auditory-Kinesthetic-Visual	1. Hearing & Saying 2. Experiencing & Doing 3. Seeing & Showing	Very verbal; high energy; good with language; learns with discussion & lecture; often interrupts; little eye contact
Auditory-Visual-Kinesthetic	1. Hearing & Saying 2. Seeing & Showing 3. Experiencing & Doing	Very verbal; good vocabulary; learns through discussion & lecture; may learn through reading; maintains eye contact
Kinesthetic-Visual-Auditory	1. Experiencing & Doing 2. Seeing & Showing 3. Hearing & Saying	Learns through hands-on; gives eye contact; good at sports; difficulty with oral reading & reports; difficulty with expressing feelings verbally
Kinesthetic-Auditory-Visual	1. Experiencing & Doing 2. Hearing & Saying 3. Seeing & Showing	Learns physically or through hands-on; difficulty sitting still; good at teaching activities; good at sports

characteristics when one looks at a single preferred modality or a combination, particularly when one looks at the first two sensory preferences. For instance, both my husband and my daughter are kinesthetic learners. Yet, they are different in some obvious ways. Marnie is KAV (Kinesthetic-Auditory-Visual). She moves and then she talks. She wiggles and jiggles. In order to learn, she must be up and moving. Scott, on the other hand, is KVA (Kinesthetic-Visual-Auditory). He learns through doing, doesn't talk much, and finds it very difficult to give formal speeches or read aloud. I believe the awareness of this information can be helpful in dealing with different learners.

THE NEED TO KNOW

There are several ways to identify your students' modalities. Understanding one's sensory preferences is a step toward metacognition and lifelong learning. The more your students know about themselves, the better learners they will be. Explain the different learning styles to them. Not only will they be fascinated, but you can help them decide which way is best and most comfortable for them to learn and study. Think of this information as a springboard rather than a crutch. Once your students lead with their strengths, they can then explore different ways of learning.

The most reliable method of identifying sensory preferences is observation. Between your careful examination and the students' own feelings about it, you can be fairly accurate in determining a preference. I have included an assessment to give your students, but it is limiting. Giving a written test to a student who does not do well on a written test can give false information. I have kept this assessment as simple as possible so that you may use it just to discuss with your students.

What Kind of Learner Are You?

Answer the following questions by choosing the response that feels the most comfortable to you.

1. When I watch a television show, I most remember
   a. the costumes, scenery, and the actor/actresses.
   b. what the characters say to each other.
   c. the action in the show or how it makes me feel.

2. When I am alone, I like to
   a. read or watch television.
   b. talk on the telephone.
   c. play a game or go outside and play.

3. If I buy my own clothes, I usually buy
   a. light-colored clothing in popular styles.
   b. bright-colored clothing.
   c. very comfortable clothing.

4. When I remember previous vacations, I most remember
   a. the way the places looked.
   b. the sounds and the conversations I had there.
   c. the way it felt to be there and the activities.

5. My favorite way to learn something is to
   a. have someone show me a picture or see it in a book.
   b. have someone tell me how to do it.
   c. do it myself.

6. When I study, I like
   a. to have soft music playing and lots of light.
   b. to have absolute silence and sometimes read aloud.
   c. to be real comfortable—like on a bed or a couch.

7. My favorite kind of class is when the teacher
   a. uses the overhead or board a lot and I can copy down the information.
   b. tells us the information and I can just listen.
   c. lets us try to do the stuff ourselves.

8. When I spell a word, I
   a. picture the word in my head.
   b. sound out the letters.
   c. write it down and see if it feels right.

9. I
   a. think talking on the phone is okay, but I'd rather see someone to talk to them.
   b. love to talk on the phone.
   c. would rather be out doing something than talk on the phone.

10. The most uncomfortable situation for me would be
    a. to not be able to watch television or read.
    b. to not be able to talk.
    c. to not be able to move around.

After having the students write down their answers, have them add up the number of a's, then the number of b's they have, and finally the number of c's. If they have mostly a's, they favor their visual modality. If they have mostly b's, it appears they favor being auditory. If the c's are their highest, then they lean toward being kinesthetic. You will find many of your students are balanced. This is helpful to them as that balance allows them to receive information in many ways; however, rest assured that in a tough situation they have a preferred modality that they will rely upon. When that situation occurs, observe carefully what modality they choose, and share your information with the student at an appropriate time.

Never let your students use their sensory preference as an excuse for inappropriate behavior! This is great information and a wonderful tool that can increase awareness of how to work on modifying your teaching and your students' learning. However, it is no reason for disrupting the class.

Jason was an eighth grader who showed an auditory preference. In fact, Jason had to talk about content in order to understand it. I started the year off talking to my students about their brains and their sensory preferences. It had always been obvious that Jason learned best by listening and speaking, and once this was confirmed I found myself less likely to reprimand Jason when he spoke—unless he disrupted the class. He started using the new information as permission to speak whenever he wanted, including when I was speaking to the class. "But Mrs. Sprenger, I can't help it. I'm an auditory learner." We had a private conversation about how his preference would be honored as long as he didn't disturb others' learning.

Okay, so you think you have a pretty good handle on how your students learn. What should you do about it? As I stress in every class, the first thing to do is to design every lesson as a VAK (Visual-Auditory-Kinesthetic) lesson. Teach your lesson three ways:

1. Use the chalkboard, overhead, hand-outs, PowerPoint, etc.

2. Give students the opportunity to talk about it.

3. Use some kind of movement or activity.

Do not panic over the kinesthetic activity! Usually some simple movements will satisfy your kinesthetic learners. So, try some dyads, triads, or other teamwork. You could simply have them stand up and share. Remember, writing *is* a kinesthetic activity—but don't overuse it. Writing on small chalk boards or dry erase boards sometimes keeps kinesthetic learners on task and up to speed.

RETEACHING

The test of all of this begins the moment you start. After you've taught the lesson, be sure to get your students started on a follow-up assignment *in class.* Sit down at your desk and see who either raises a hand for a question or comes up to your desk. These are the students who missed something.

Students in your classroom who have difficulty encoding information the way you give it are the "translators." What actually is going on in their brains is called a *cross modal transfer.* We all do these transfers at times. For instance, you reach into your pocket and find a small round object. From feeling this object you get the picture in your mind of a coin. From the size, you determine that it is a quarter. These students take your information and translate from your modality to their own. Many people are very good at this transfer; however, information can be lost in the process. It may appear that these students are not paying attention, yet they may have been working very diligently at the transfer and simply missed some of the message.

As you find yourself reteaching these students, pay close attention to how they are finally "getting it." Do they need you to literally draw them a picture? Do they need you to explain it again, verbally? Or perhaps it helps them if they show you how they think it should be and you correct it as they go along? Discover the modality of students you are reaching the least and plan to hit that one harder in your lessons. Eventually, you will find that very little or no reteaching will be necessary. And because you are "speaking the same language" as your students, they will feel they are significant in your class. You will see healthy self-esteem grow in your room.

I have had some great successes dealing with sensory preferences. These experiences have motivated me to continue researching all of these techniques.

An eighth grader in my homeroom has had some real difficulties all of her life because of her auditory-kinesthetic-visual preference. Erin struggled with her need to hear and feel (externally) that she was succeeding.

I often told Erin to roam around the classroom at different times in order to meet her kinesthetic needs, and frequently sent a group of auditory learners, including Erin, into another room to read stories aloud for literature. During a discussion in class one day, I discovered another area that was a problem for Erin. It started when I asked the question, "How many of you have turned off the radio or an iron and then had to go back and check to see if you had really turned it off?" In checking for this external reinforcer, I had opened a real can of worms!

"Mrs. Sprenger, you wouldn't believe how many times Erin has to go all the way back upstairs to check to see if her curling iron is off!" announced Susan, a close friend of Erin's.

"Oh, yes, Mrs. Sprenger, I've waited for her in the car several times because she has to check and recheck her room," shouted another excited eighth grader.

Erin sat very still, very red-faced, and nodded in agreement. "I just don't trust myself to know that I did it," was her meek response to the barrage of criticism from well-meaning friends who had wanted to complain about this for some time. As the discussion continued and the topic changed, I took the information about Erin and tucked it away for later study.

The next day I took Erin aside. I told her that I might have some information to help her. I first explained to her that because of her auditory-kinesthetic preferences, looking at the curling iron as she turned it off did not give her a sense of completion. I instructed her to do two things. First of all, I told her that after she turns off the curling iron she must say aloud to herself, "Yes, Erin!" or "Good job, Erin!" She must use her name and she must say it aloud, at least initially. Second, she must, at the same time she is talking to herself, do something physically to show completion. She could clap her hands or use the hand signal from the movie *Home Alone* (where the youngster puts his arm in front of him with clenched fist and pulls it toward him with a "Yes!").

Erin began using this system that evening. As of this writing, Erin no longer has to check to see if the curling iron is off, or the radio, or anything else. After the first two weeks of trying this method, she learned how to complete that success cycle with an appropriate reinforcer.

This carried over into her studying. She now knows when she knows. She gives herself similar reinforcement when she studies for a test and when she is taking a test. She never used to have the feeling that she was really finished answering a question until she discovered how to convince herself. This external convincer eventually became an *internal* convincer for Erin.

ALL PATHWAYS LEAD TO DIFFERENTIATION

This is one approach to differentiating the classroom. I feel that it is one of the more important approaches as it relates directly to memory. I am not referring here to memorization.

Memorization within the context of education is often looked upon with distaste. However, memorization is necessary for learning, and I find that most teachers are eager to learn memory strategies to use with their students. By using strategies associated with specific sensory pathways in the brain, teachers can help students make associations and teach them lifelong learning techniques.

DIFFERENT STROKES

1. Playing Simon Says is a wonderful way to include all senses. Interestingly, those who have a visual preference are most likely to make mistakes. It is a great way to allow students to see the importance of using all of the senses.

2. Mind mapping is another excellent way to utilize VAK. Have students create mind maps for review in their groups: Students put the main idea in the middle of a sheet of paper and draw a cloud around it. For each supporting detail, have students draw lines from the cloud in different colors. On each line have them briefly write the detail, and close by create a symbol or picture representing the information. This allows conversation for the auditory preference, movement for the kinesthetic, and plenty of words and symbols for the visual. It's a great review tool! For additional instructions on mind mapping read *Head First* by Tony Buzan (2002), the creator of this organizational system.

A Matter
of Memory

3

Janice is talking to Margo when I arrive early one morning. They are standing in the hallway outside Margo's room.

"And I just can't believe it," Janice says. "That was the best unit I ever taught. The kids worked in teams. I used multi-sensory teaching strategies. We played games. We did role plays. We had puppet shows. I was so excited as I watched every student really get involved."

"Hey, this is a conversation I want to hear," I said. "Sounds like the plan is working."

"Well, I thought so," Janice continues, "but I was wrong. I don't know how I messed up."

"It doesn't sound like you messed up. What do you mean?"

"I gave the kids the test on the unit. I thought they'd all do great. But the scores are really low! What's wrong with them? Were they just pretending to be involved?"

I smile, knowingly. "I've heard this song before. In fact, I've sung it. It's happened to both of us, too."

Margo nods. "You need to know about memory and how it works. Once you understand that, you'll be able to avoid this problem and several others."

"Memory?" Janice asks. "Are you telling me that these young kids can't remember?"

"Not exactly," Margo replies. "There's much more to it than that."

We have all experienced what Janice was going through. You think you have the perfect unit. The students are involved. They're motivated. And you all are having fun learning. It seems that this is what school should be about. And it is.

Neuroscientists tell us that one way to link research to the classroom is through memory (Peterson, 2000; Zola, 2002). But memory is tricky. You know that. You've probably "lost" your car keys, forgotten someone's name, or been heading to the grocery store and ended up at work! The brain is a marvelous organ, and it's been discovered that memory is not just one thing; some neuroscientists, like Candace Pert, believe that we store memories throughout our bodies (Pert, 1997). As educators we want to pour information into our students' heads and pray that it will stay there. We have, however, more than one kind of memory, and some types work better for us than others. My goal has always been to help students discover which memory pathway works best for them for the topic we are covering. This is truly metacognition.

I am deep into a chapter of my book. The phone interrupts my concentration. It is my daughter, Marnie.

"Hey, Mom!" she shouts into my ear, "I'm making dinner for Dan (the current boyfriend). I'm going to make those noodles you make from scratch, but I can't remember the recipe. Will you give it to me?"

Any thoughts of the book are out the window and I start scanning my brain for recipes. "Sure. Do you have a pencil?"

I list the ingredients for my daughter. "Once you put all of that together, you have to knead the dough."

"I've never done that before. How do I do it?" She sounds a little panicky.

"No problem. It's simple. You just take the dough out of the pan and put it on a cutting board. Be sure to flour the board first." I hesitate as my mind takes me to the kitchen and the last time I made the noodles.

"Then what?" Marnie demands.

"Then you sort of pat it . . ." I put down my book. I look at my hands and try to picture myself kneading. I start over. "Place the dough on a well-floured, flat surface, grab the side of the dough farthest away from you and fold it toward yourself. Sort of fold the dough in half and use the heel of your hand to push the dough into itself."

"Wait a minute, Mom. Maybe I better call you back when I'm ready to do it."

"That's fine. You know, you're going to need a lot of flour on that board because the dough is going to be sticky. . . . Maybe I'll make some noodles, too, so I can walk you through this more easily!"

It was difficult for me to explain to Marnie the procedure for kneading dough. I'll even go one step farther—it was uncomfortable. I knew it would be simple if we just did it together. The reason for my discomfort was not a flaw in my brain (although there are probably quite a few!). My discomfort stemmed from the fact that I had not stored this particular information in the memory pathway that I was trying to utilize. I was attempting to take a "how to" memory and make it a "know that" memory. The file in my brain for kneading dough was somehow connected to my fingers—I needed to actually perform the procedure to get the words to come into my head.

PHASES OF MEMORY

Memory researchers discuss three phases of memory. They are the learning or encoding phase, the storage phase, and the retrieval phase (Squire & Kandel, 1999). Problems can occur at any one of these phases. For instance, the learning phase can be interrupted by lack of attention, focus, or concentration. We have learned the importance of sleep in storing information (Wilson & McNaughton, 1994). Sleep deprivation can prevent the storage phase from operating. Lack of appropriate cues, distortion of information, and just plain forgetting can cause problems in the retrieval phase (Schacter, 2001).

CATEGORIZING MEMORY

When one looks at memory, generally three processes come to mind: sensory memory, short-term memory processes consisting of immediate and active working memory, and long-term memory. Before we can even begin to understand why I couldn't easily verbalize how to make those noodles, we must have a basic understanding of these memory forms.

Sensory Memory

All information enters our brains through our senses. We therefore deal with visual, auditory, kinesthetic, olfactory, and gustatory information. In other words, our perception of the world comes in the form of sights, sounds, touches, smells, and tastes. This information is sent to appropriate areas in our brains, called association cortices, in the top layer of the brain, the cortex. It is here that information is identified.

Sensory memory is fleeting. Joseph LeDoux describes the association areas as sensory buffers. Information is held in these areas from milliseconds to seconds (LeDoux, 1996). This is long enough for our incredible brains to get a perception of what we are experiencing in each of these senses. Then this information, as described in the previous chapter, is sent to the rhinal cortex, a convergence zone. The sensory messages converge and form a representation. Does this quest ever fail? There may be times when the sensory information does not make sense, so the representation is not clear. If this were to happen, that particular memory would be dropped by the brain. The rhinal cortex sends the information to the hippocampus for further representation. Here it may also be conceptualized (LeDoux, 2002). (See Figure 3.1.)

Let's use the television commercial about the brain and drugs. The original commercial showed an egg with the line, "This is your brain." Then it showed an egg being fried and said, "This is your brain on drugs." This visual and auditory information entered our brains. It was sent to the thalamus, which acted like Grand Central Station by sending the information to the appropriate cortex. The sights and the sounds were identified in these association cortices. Then the information was relayed to the rhinal cortex where it came together as the single representation that we recognize. The rhinal cortex sends the information to the hippocampus. Here, the brain is able not only to know that it is seeing a comparison between a whole egg and a fried egg, but with the help of the frontal lobes of the brain, it also is able to make the abstract connection to the brain being "fried" on drugs. If this information is going to be stored in long-term memory, the hippocampus sends it back to the sensory cortex where it originated for storage.

Immediate Memory

Immediate memory is the process by which the sensory memory just discussed is held in the brain. Sometimes this memory is called *conscious* memory. George Miller researched this area in the 1950s, and from his work it has long been thought that this process allows us to hold up to seven bits of information (Baddeley, 1999). Recently, however, this work is being challenged. The "magical number seven" has been reduced to

Figure 3.1

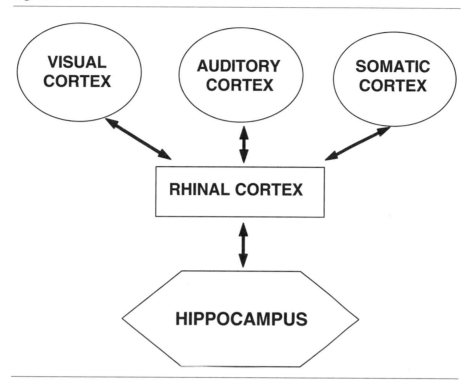

four. According to some new studies, the brain has a more limited capacity for immediate memory than was proposed by Miller. Cowan (2001) concludes that adult capacity for this short-term storage is between three and five bits of information.

Immediate memory holds information for a short period of time. It allows us to take in new information and hold it while more is added. Ideally, we then make connections with this information and can hold onto more. Each bit of information may be called a chunk. Sometimes we can hold only very small chunks of information. For instance, I remember when I was first introduced to my Palm Pilot. As my son was explaining it to me, I could take in only a few pieces of information at a time. After I became accustomed to the simpler processes, he could tell me more and I could hold onto bigger chunks of Palm Pilot information. It is said that the difference between an expert and a novice is that the size of the chunks of information are much larger for the expert (Squire & Kandel, 1999).

Active Working Memory

This memory process is a type of short-term memory; it is between immediate and long-term memory. Active working memory performs different tasks that are very important for school success. This is where new information and old information meet (Levine, 2002). As we are exposed to new material, our brains try to make sense of it by looking for "hooks" that are already established. If we can hang the information on one of these hooks, we are much more likely to remember it.

According to Levine (2000), active working memory participates in our memory process by

- Acting as a storage area to compare and combine a new memory with old memories

- Storing the first words of a sentence so you understand the gist of it when you get to the end

- Holding information as you use strategies to remember it

- Holding parts of problems as you solve them

- Retaining a question as your mind searches for an answer

Immediate memory can hold information without rehearsal for a matter of seconds. With elaboration, the process switches to active working memory that can hold information for an indefinite amount of time. This information will not necessarily go into long-term memory unless some meaning is made from it. We all can remember staying up the night before an exam and "cramming." This process holds information in active working memory. It does not usually form the connections for a long-term memory. We realize this as we leave the exam and promptly forget what we have studied.

Four factors that affect immediate and working memory are particularly important for learning (Hopper, 2000). They are the following:

- Interest
- Intent
- Understanding
- Prior knowledge

Our students should be aware of these four aspects of memory. If the interest, understanding, and prior knowledge are not present, then intent—the student must intend to remember—can make the difference. That intent can translate into using a specific memory lane that the student finds easy to use.

Figure 3.2   Information from the environment goes into sensory buffer zones to be recognized. This lasts for no longer than about four seconds before it decays or moves into immediate memory. Then the information either is dropped, lost through interference, or moves on to active working memory. If the information makes sense and has meaning, it will go to long-term memory.

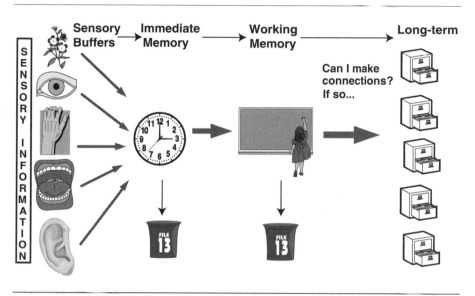

SOURCE: Adapted from the Atkinson & Shiffrin (1968) model of information processing

Long-Term Memory

Long-term memory is divided into two types: implicit and explicit. Implicit, sometimes called nondeclarative, is memory that occurs without conscious effort. Explicit, sometimes called declarative, is conscious memory. Joseph LeDoux (2002) describes explicit memory as having two components: semantic memory and episodic memory. He then divides implicit memory into four components: conditioning, skills, priming, and other. Emotional memory is usually included as an implicit memory system. For our purposes, I follow LeDoux's format for explicit memory, but I divide implicit memory into conditioned response, procedural (skills), and emotional memory.

EXPLICIT MEMORY

Explicit or declarative memory is the memory for facts and events. It can be consciously retrieved and can be declared—put into words. Semantic

Figure 3.3

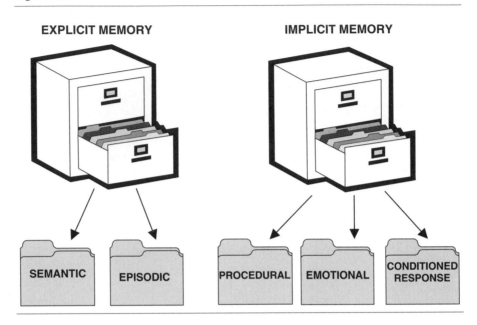

and episodic are the two memory pathways in this category. Since we have been referring to sensory passageways and pathways, I will refer to the memory pathways as memory lanes. Educational curriculum utilizes these explicit lanes more often than the implicit lanes. Explicit memory requires the use of the short-term and working memory processes. These involve the brain structure, the hippocampus, and it is necessary for the filing of new factual memories (Bourtchouladze, 2002).

How Do We Deal With Explicit Information?

One of the most difficult aspects of teaching is making those necessary connections between the content and the real world. When I am training educators, one of the most frequently asked questions is, "What do I say to my students when they ask how my content is ever going to be useful to them? I'm not sure it will be!" Read the following example.

The Goopation of Garpon

To survive in this world, everyone must be familiar with garpon. In order to use garpon successfully, it must be goopated often. Goopation begins with oxporation. Oxporation can only take place once every proquar. To oxporate, you must mix zorzine with cafon and stir gently. When the oxporation is complete, add garpon and the mixture will spontaneously goopate. Goopation can take from 12 to 14 spomanes. You will know the garpon is goopated when it fuzzles.

1. What do you need to survive in this world?

2. How does goopation begin?

3. What do you need to oxporate?

4. How does the mixture goopate?

5. How long does goopation take?

6. How will you know when the garpon is goopated?

SOURCE: Adapted from *The Montillation of Traxoline* by Pat Wolfe (1996).

Could you answer the questions at the end? Of course. Did you learn anything? No. The reason is simple. You have no prior knowledge of garpon. There are no "hooks" in your brain to hang this information on. My guess is that you could take this information home and study it, take a test on it tomorrow, and get an "A." Then will you have learned something? No. With no hooks for the information, you would work with it in active working memory, take the test, and then forget the information.

Yet we consistently do this with students. We teach them, test them, and assume they have learned something if they have passed the test. Here's my belief:

- Some of what we teach is garpon to all of our students!
- All of what we teach is garpon to some of our students!
- A large part of our job is to make garpon memorable!

Semantic Memory: Nothing But the Facts

A great deal of the information presented to students is processed through the semantic memory lane. Semantic memory is general factual memory and must be processed consciously for retention. Teaching strategies for semantic information include using mnemonic devices (Keefe, 1997). The brain may have trouble holding information if it has very little meaning to the learner or if the learner can't get a "hook" into the content. Acrostics, acronyms, and peg systems help provide that hook.

The students are waiting for the lesson to begin. It's time for a new unit and we have many vocabulary words with which to become familiar. I arrange the students in teams. Each team is given the list of new vocabulary words. Before I finish distributing them, one of my traditional learners asks, "Should we look these up and write them in our notebooks?"

I respond, "Today we are going to do something different with these words. With your teammates, take each word on the list and connect it to a pencil. For instance, the first word on your list is 'carpetbaggers.' These are Northerners who moved south during and after the Civil War to make their fortunes. They carried suitcases made of carpet material. How can we connect the word carpetbaggers with a pencil?"

"You mean, like, 'The carpetbaggers used the pencil to add up all the money they were making in the south'?" responded one student.

"How about, 'The carpetbaggers wrote their names on their bags of carpet with a pencil so they could identify which bag belonged to them'?" said another.

"Both of those answers will work. Continue with your teams to finish the list."

When I ask the students to share their definitions of the words and how they connected them to a pencil, an amazing thing happens. They know all the definitions without having to read from their papers. The *pencil* provided the hook that their brains needed to remember the words.

This memory strategy gave my students the opportunity to form a connection in their brains where they may not otherwise have had one. With a firm grasp of the vocabulary, my students were ready to use complex cognitive skills such as synthesis and evaluation. The basic knowledge was in place to enable higher thinking.

Other ways of processing semantic information include mind mapping, debating, and role playing.

Episodic Memory: Making the Invisible Visible

Episodic memory is location and circumstance related (Bourtchouladze, 2002). We remember a place and recall what was learned there. When asked to recall what you did yesterday, your brain first tries to discover where you were. With that information, you can draw on the activities, the people involved, and even how you felt about them.

If a student is having trouble recalling previously learned material, it may be that the information is encoded in his brain, but he needs the appropriate trigger to find it (Squire & Kandel, 1999). Bulletin boards, posters, sounds, smells, and tastes can all help stimulate these kinds of memories. Our classrooms must become unique sites of learning. Assessment can be enhanced by testing in the same room where the learning took place (Gregory & Chapman, 2002).

Teachers are covered with invisible information. Have you ever seen a student stare at you while taking a test? She is probably trying to get a mental picture of you teaching the material to help access the information.

IMPLICIT MEMORY

Implicit memory includes memories that are not consciously learned (Schacter, 2001). They are more involved with feelings and "how to" rather than the "what" of explicit memory. Implicit or nondeclarative memories include conditioned response, and emotional and procedural memory lanes. Information that is placed in these memory lanes does not have to go through the short-term memory processes.

Conditioned Response: Lasting Memories

If I say, "Plop, plop, fizz, fizz . . ." those who are old enough will reply, "oh, what a relief it is!" Why do we have this frivolous information permanently stored in our minds? Because it became lodged there by repetition, and the process of repetition forms strong networks in the brain. Some conditioned responses require a trigger, and others, such as decoding skills, multiplication tables, and the alphabet, do not. Why not use this incredible memory lane to help our students remember?

For example, students can take material from a unit and put it to a melody or a rhythm. They must choose the information to include, estimate the amount of time it will take to say or sing, and use their imaginations to create this work. You are giving them choices as to what the final product will be and giving them an excellent chance to problem solve. This is a wonderful brain-based lesson.

One of the data-supported strategies in *Classroom Instruction That Works* (Marzano, 2001a) is the use of metaphor. It is a powerful way to help kids remember. They can make the metaphor themselves (ownership helps memory) and attach details to it. The steps to creating metaphors can be practiced and used with any grade level.

Figure 3.4

Creating Metaphors

- Choose two unlike elements. (brain and pudding)

- Examine literal definitions. (brain—most complex organ in the human body/pudding—a sweet treat that you look forward to having)

- Determine how they are alike in the literal view. (You have to have a brain to appreciate the pudding.)

- Find an abstract connection. (Even though the pudding sets, just like the brain, it can be changed.)

SOURCE: Adapted from *Handbook for Classroom Instruction That Works* (Marzano, 2002).

Procedural Memory: Just Do it!

"Hey, Mrs. Sprenger, Erin and I know all about the brain. We made up a brain cheer! Want to see it?"

They have my complete attention. Brain Awareness Week is just around the corner. The girls have been studying the brain in their science class.

They hold up their hands with fingers spread and begin: They clap once and then hold up their hands again. "Neurons listen with their dendrites," they chant. As they say this, they first wiggle their fingers, and then use their hands to pull on their ears, and again hold up their hands and wiggle their fingers, and then they clap three times. Continuing, they chant, "Neurons talk through their axons," and with this they hold up their hands, then point with both hands to their mouths, and take each hand and rub the opposite forearm (indicating the axon). They clap three times again. "Messages go in the dendrites, down the axon, swim across the synapse to the next neuron." As they chant this, they wiggle their fingers, rub down each forearm, use swimming motions with their arms, and end with fingers wiggling. I am impressed, and I ask the girls to teach the rest of the class.

Procedural memory is convincing. It often gets us to work in the morning when we aren't quite awake. This memory is frequently called muscle memory, and its storage area is also the cerebellum. It feels like the learning is not in our heads, but rather in our bodies. Since this type of memory storage works well, it is a plus to use in the classroom. Research suggests how potent movement is to learning by requiring some decision making, engaging emotions, and encouraging socialization (Jensen, 2000b). Creating procedures for all learning would be difficult. Yet for some learning, procedural memory is simple and necessary. Adding simple hand movements, like clapping, to semantic information adds another pathway for the learning. I have watched many students doing the hand motions quietly while they retrieve information for an assessment.

Nonmotor procedural memory includes many processes that do not require "muscle memory," yet still are ways of doing things (Levine, 2002). There is a small structure at the bottom of the brain called the cerebellum. It is this structure that allows us to perform motor and nonmotor tasks without thinking about them. Then we can tend to specific details or creative ideas with our active working memory (Leiner & Leiner, 1997). Nonmotor procedures include how to head a paper, the proper steps in solving a math problem, and the format for letter writing.

Emotional Memory: If They Can Feel It, They'll Remember It!

This memory lane is the most powerful. Neutral experiences leave little to remember. Emotionally laden experiences are sometimes kept throughout life. Emotions affect attention, perception, decision making, and memory (LeDoux, 2002). Since this is such a dominant factor in memory, educators must make the most of emotion in the classroom. Balance is the key here. Too much emotional stimuli will interfere with memory formation; too little and the experience is quickly forgotten.

Facilitating emotional memory can be a challenge for teachers. Since this is the most powerful pathway, it must be given great consideration. Emotional memory is stored through the brain structure called the amygdala. As I stated in the information processing model in Chapter 1, the amygdala filters incoming information for emotional content. This emotional center is an aggressive force in the brain (McEwen & Lasley, 2002).

Sometimes our own excitement will generate some emotion in our students. But the best way to get at their emotions is to personalize the learning. We remember stories more easily than simple facts. Taking semantic information and putting it into story form can be quite time-consuming for teachers—but it's great for the students. Assigning chapters or chunks of information to teams of students and challenging them to put it in story form offers endless possibilities. Again, students must synthesize and evaluate. They use creative-thinking skills and problem solve because they must develop a story that makes sense and relates important information. They take ownership of their work and therefore of the learning. It is a wonderful product for assessment and it also prepares them for a traditional assessment if you choose. Students are eager to evaluate and discuss stories written by classmates. The learning becomes personalized.

Debates, role plays, puppet shows, and skits add emotion to learning. They can add a real-life association to learning as well (Sylwester, 2000). Relating assessment to the activities or referring to the activities in a written assessment will aid in retrieval.

STROLLING DOWN MEMORY LANES FOR PRIOR KNOWLEDGE

Accessing prior knowledge through memory storage is also an option. When I introduce a unit, I try each pathway to jog my students' memories. I always begin with emotions, since the emotional pathway is the strongest.

Emotional: How do you feel about _____?

Episodic: Where did you find out about _____?

Procedural: How do you use _____?

Semantic: What do you know about _____?

Conditioned Response: For this pathway, the students may not have anything stored. I often ask them to create a metaphor for the topic if they have any prior knowledge in the other pathways. (For instance, *mythology is a soap opera.*)

MAKING CONNECTIONS

As students start to understand their memory lanes, they will learn how their own brains work best. Actively monitoring and regulating their cognitive processes provides students with some control over their learning. Many who have had difficulty learning and remembering may find a lane that works better for them. They literally have the tools to rewire their brains. Offering opportunities to encode information through different memory systems helps students feel successful about learning and gives them strategies to use throughout their lives. Assisting them in transferring information from one lane to another allows them to make the associations they need for complex cognitive thinking and problem solving. Finally, matching

Figure 3.5

Memory Lane	Strategy	Transfer
Procedural	Use body parts for food pyramid	Practice saying *food pyramid* without movement; encourage students to visualize movement
Episodic	Museum field trip for art	Review and debrief trip after return; refer to trip location on assessment
Conditioned Response	Song	Question students about information in the song; refer to the song on the assessment
Emotional	Celebration before learning	Recreate the celebration before assessment; refer to emotions on assessment

assessments to the memory lanes will allow students to demonstrate their knowledge and skills.

The problem Janice was having with her students and assessment was simply a mismatch. She had taught the material using most of the memory lanes. Since she was unaware that she was doing this, her assessment was the traditional paper-and-pencil test. There is nothing wrong with this type of assessment, but this was not what Janice had prepared her students for. In other words, she had helped her students store information in procedural memory (with puppet shows), episodic memory (costumes, posters, accessories), conditioned response (songs, poems, metaphors), and emotional memory (excitement, celebration, personalization), and then she tested them in the semantic lane.

Transfer does not automatically take place. In fact, every time you use a memory lane other than semantic, you must practice the transfer if you are giving a semantic assessment. What does this look like? (See Figure 3.5.)

DIFFERENTIATION

Just as students have sensory preferences, they may have some strong memory preferences, as well (Small, 2002). As each long-term memory pathway is addressed, a different way of learning is offered. The teacher becomes a guide or facilitator, and students explore how their memories work. I have often found that some of my special education students have difficulty using semantic memory. Procedural memory works better for them. They can remember information best with their bodies. The movement becomes automatic and they no longer have to explicitly retrieve information. When working on some of our science experiments, these students would practice the lab steps over and over. When they were tested on this information, they conjured a mental picture of what they had done, step by step.

The futurists believe that our students will change careers—not jobs, careers—between 10 and 14 times in their lives. We have no idea what jobs to prepare them for. They need to have basic knowledge and the ability to learn as each new career presents itself. Understanding how their memory works, and how it works best, can make them lifelong learners with an advantage.

MAKING GARPON MEMORABLE

In an effort to have nonsense make sense, I offered my students the opportunity to make garpon memorable. Here are two interesting and fun results.

Automatic Memory

(Sung to the tune of "Clementine")

Goopate your garpon,
Goopate your garpon
very often, just like so.
Take the zorzine, add the cafon,
and stir gently don't you know.
Oxporation only takes place
Every proquar, so take care
Watch the timer and on the proquar
Begin the process if you dare.
Add your garpon to the mixture
and spontaneously
After 12 to 14 spomanes
it will goopate properly.
You will be finished when it fuzzles
and then you will be glad,
Because being without garpon
would be very, very sad.

Emotional/Episodic

Everyone Should Be Familiar With Garpon: Is That Your Final Answer?

"Twelve to fourteen spomanes? I can't wait that long! I have to catch my flight. I guess I'll have to go without my garpon," moaned George.

"Where are you going?" asked Guy, the garpon guy.

"I'm going to be on TV with Regis Philbin. I want to be a millionaire!" George said proudly. He left Guy, the garpon guy, and flew to the show.

The fast fingers question was easy for George. It was such a surprise to see garpon questions on the show. The question was, "Put the garpon processes in order beginning with the first step. (A) fuzzling (B) oxporation (C) goopation. George did it quickly. He knew that in order to goopate garpon, you had to begin with oxporation. Then it had to fuzzle before it would be goopated. He quickly punched in B, A, C.

"George from Peoria is our winner!" shouted Reg. "Come over here, George. Are you ready to play?"

"I was born ready!" yelled George.

"Then let's begin with your first question. For $100, what two things do you need for the process of oxporation: (A) salt and pepper, (B) vinegar and oil, (C) cafon and zorzine, or D) Mutt and Jeff?"

George began to panic. His heart raced. Why couldn't he get this one? "I thought the $100 questions were supposed to be easy," he said to Regis in a shaky voice.

"Well, the studio thinks everyone should be familiar with garpon," said Regis. "So we thought you would know about oxporation. Do you want to use a lifeline?"

"I guess I'll poll the audience," George said, a little embarrassed.

"Okay, audience, press your buttons!" shouted Regis.

"The audience is 100% in favor of (C) cafon and zorzine!" Regis announced.

"Okay, I'll trust the audience and take (C) cafon and zorzine."

"Is that your final answer?" asked Regis.

"Final answer."

"You're right! Now you'll go for $200. Here's the question: Garpon is goopated when it (A) fizzles, (B) fuzzles, (C) whistles, or (D) boils."

"Oh, no, Reg, another hard one!" moaned George. "I need another lifeline. Let's do the fifty/fifty."

"Okay. Please take two answers away, leaving one incorrect answer and the correct answer. George, you are left with (A) fizzles and (B) fuzzles. What is your final answer?"

"My final answer is B."

"And you are right for $200! For $300, here is your question. How does garpon goopate? (A) sporadically, (B) carefully, (C) spontaneously, or (D) reluctantly?"

"How come all the garpon questions? This doesn't seem fair," George was very upset. "I'll have to use my last lifeline. I'd like to call Rosie O'Donnell."

"Okay, AT&T will get Rosie on the phone . . . Rosie? This is Regis Philbin. George is here and needs your help. Go ahead, George."

"Rosie, How does garpon goopate? Sporadically, carefully, spontaneously, or reluctantly?"

"Oh, George, this is easy. I can't believe you don't know it. It's spontaneously, trust me. If it's wrong, I'll give you twice as much money!"

"Okay, I'll go with C, spontaneously."

"You're right!!! You have no lifelines left. You have been such a good sport we are going to jump to the million-dollar question. Are you ready?"

"I guess."

"Okay, here it is. How long does it take garpon to goopate? (A) 2 to 4 spomanes, (B) 5 to 7 spomanes, (C) 10 to 12 spomanes, or (D) 12 to 14 spomanes?"

George suddenly smiled. He thought of Guy, the garpon guy. "I know this one—it's (D) 12 to 14 spomanes!"

"Is that your final answer?"

"That is my final answer," George said confidently.

"You're right! You've just become a millionaire!"

And that is why everyone should be familiar with garpon.

DIFFERENT STROKES

1. Learning centers can be set up according to memory lanes. They can each contain the content in a different manner. A fourth-grade teacher uses this idea when she does her weather unit.

Conditioned Response Center: At this center, students find weather songs and poems to read and discuss. They also write weather songs.

Episodic Center: This center is for creating posters and pictures of weather to hang in the room.

Emotional Center: Personal stories of weather disasters and triumphs are read and watched on video.

Procedural Center: At this center, students learn the plans and techniques for dealing with different weather situations.

Semantic Center: Books and articles about weather are provided. Students make up mnemonic devices to help them remember. Pictures are drawn of several weather conditions.

This teacher found that, although the students could choose which centers to use, they all wanted to experience each one.

2. Mr. Fuller, a middle school math teacher, was intrigued with memory research and wanted to experiment with differentiation in this way. He offered some authentic assessments via memory lanes.

Episodic: Students were offered the opportunity to set up field explorations with local businesses. These mini-internships were either videotaped or audiotaped.

Procedural: Students could devise techniques for alternative problem solving and teach them to the class.

Semantic: Students could create mind maps or other nonlinguistic representations of the problem-solving techniques.

Conditioned response: Metaphors could be created and expanded upon.

Emotional: The key to this learning would be a story or scenario that would have strong emotional content and relate to other students in a way to make it memorable.

What Mr. Fuller liked most about these activities was the fact that the students were talking math. They dialogued about each product and presentation and concluded that more than one memory lane was probably necessary for full understanding of the problem and solution. Great reflection and metacognition!

Differentiation Design

4

Remembering Visual Information

It's Friday afternoon. Margo, Janice, and I are helping MaryAnn, the eighth-grade language arts teacher, with tryouts for the school play. We've just heard our fifth Romeo and our sixth Juliet. After this long week, we can barely tell them apart.

"Have you seen the new eighth-grade boy?" MaryAnn asks.

Janice and Margo shake their heads "no," but I respond, "Yes, he was in my study hall this afternoon. I think they're still trying to figure out his schedule. What's he like?"

"Well, he seems very nice, but you know he has been expelled from a few schools. No one seems to know what the problem is, but I noticed something today. I asked the kids to copy a paragraph from the board. It was on the story that we read today, and it took him forever. He was working at it, too. He would look at the board, write down a word, then look back up, and write down another. Wouldn't you think he's old enough to do better than that?"

Janice pipes up, "Sounds like a short-term memory problem to me!"

Margo and I smile at each other. "Would you like to elaborate on that?" Margo asks.

"Well, it could be a short-term visual memory problem. He may have trouble with symbols in general, and of course, he may have been trying to keep up with everyone else and that made it worse."

"So, what do I do about that?" MaryAnn asks Janice.

Janice's eyes widen. She looks at Margo and me. "Well, girls, what strategies can we come up with to help MaryAnn?"

The student in MaryAnn's class is having trouble with short-term visual memory. This is only one area that can be troublesome with this memory process. When we look up a phone number, we usually say it to ourselves until we dial it and forget it. Some students have trouble holding the visual long enough to repeat it. When students have difficulties copying from the board, they may not have any strategies to help themselves (Olivier & Bowler, 1996). Suggestions might include

- Sitting in the front of the room, close to the overhead or chalkboard

- Learning to mutter the words softly while visually moving from the board to the paper

- Practicing visualizing words (This can be done at home, too. Looking at a word, closing one's eyes, and trying to hold onto it for a few seconds.)

- Practicing forming associations

Explicit memory, semantic in particular, is the memory we deal with most often in education. In my experience of training educators, the majority of them are visual learners. Therefore, much of what our students are exposed to is semantic, visual teaching. This is great for our students who prefer the visual sensory pathway, but what about the others? Multi-sensory teaching is one answer. Another is to differentiate our teaching in the visual mode. Multi-sensory teaching will allow students to learn from their strengths, certainly an admirable way to differentiate. It is also helpful to students to work on their weaknesses so differentiating visually works well.

DO YOU TEACH FOR VISUAL MEMORY?

It may be beneficial to look at your style of teaching. If you prefer visual input, you probably also give it. Ask yourself the following questions:

1. Do I use a lot of visual aids?

2. Do I find covering a lot of material important?

3. Do I often talk fast?

4. Does messiness bother me a great deal?

5. Do I have to see it to believe it?

6. Am I easily distracted by visual stimuli? (When my students are moving or squirming, does it bother me?)

7. Do I rely on printed information?

8. Do I need visual feedback from my students (tests, etc.)?

If you answered yes to most of these, you are possibly pushing the visual format for learning. If you are balancing that with other sensory stimulation, you may be encountering fewer major problems with your students. In my diverse classrooms, I always had a few students who needed something different to help them learn.

DIFFERENTIATION DESIGN FOR LEARNERS WITH STRONG VISUAL MEMORY

When short-term memory is broken down into visual (iconic) and auditory (echoic) memories, visual memory runs a distant second to auditory memory (Baddeley, 1999). It is the visual portion of short-term memory that can hold only three to four items.

If you are a visual teacher, you appreciate what a visually oriented student requires. This student will want to actually see words written down, a picture of something being described, a time line to remember events in history, or the assignment written on the board. She will probably organize her materials. She will even appreciate being able to follow with an overhead transparency or handout. This is the student who benefits from looking at the textbook and taking notes. She may be your ideal student.

If you are not a visual teacher, this student may appear more demanding to you, or may have more difficulty in your classroom. She may need written directions as well as written explanations of diagrams, maps, and charts.

Perhaps you have read what educator Sandra Rief (1993) said about retention. Students remember

- 10% of what they read
- 20% of what they hear

- 30% of what they see
- 50% of what they see and hear
- 70% of what they say
- 90% of what they say and do

Keep this in mind as we look at individual strengths. Our students will learn and retain more if they are using many senses. With new material in particular, we all need to lead with our strongest sense and then reinforce the learning in as many ways as possible.

Visual Memory and the Semantic Lane

Semantic memory, the type of memory used for words and text, is difficult to store. It must go through the immediate and active working memory processes. Even the best visual learner may have difficulty with this memory lane. There are proven strategies that are successful for all learners, and several that the visual learner may relate to quite easily.

1. Nonlinguistic representations; drawing pictures, graphic organizers

2. Mind mapping

3. Mental pictures

4. Summarizing and note taking

5. Practice and homework

6. Time lines

For students with strong visual skills, all of the preceding may be appreciated and used easily. For those who have trouble visualizing, these strategies need to be taught in small steps. Even though "a picture may be worth a thousand words" for strong visual learners, it may be very confusing to others. Using visuals in instruction will help us take advantage of the way students entertain themselves, and may indeed influence the student from poverty who may be exposed to more television than books (Burmark, 2002). Analogies can be helpful in explaining visual information to weaker learners. These students may strengthen their visual skills through board games and puzzles.

Jordan is attempting some brain teasers during study hall. He has finished his other work, played two games of chess with a classmate, and looks frustrated as I see him turning pages back and forth.

"What are you up to, Jordan?" I inquire.

"I'm doing one of those brain teasers where they show you two pictures and you have to find seven things that are different. This is making me crazy. I can't remember for five seconds when I turn the page!"

"Jordan, attending to detail is important in this type of quiz. Are you looking carefully at the first picture?"

"I think I am, but when I turn the page and look at the other picture, I lose it!"

"Most of these challenges have the pictures together on one page, so this one is a more difficult task. Take more time and get a 'picture' of the picture in your head. In fact, you might look at it for a minute and then try writing down what you saw." To me, I see a wonderful opportunity for Jordan to increase his visual memory.

"Okay, I'll try that. But if it doesn't work, will you make a copy of the second picture so I can put them side by side?"

"You have a deal." I go back to my desk to observe from a distance. Looking over Jordan's shoulder is only going to add unnecessary stress.

A few minutes later, Jordan closes the book and puts it in his desk. The top of the desk comes down with a bang, and I look at him astonished.

"It's okay, Mrs. Sprenger, I didn't mean to make any noise. I'm finished with that book now. That last puzzle was the only one I hadn't been able to complete. Your idea worked. I just needed to take some time and think about what I saw. Writing it down really helped."

Jordan is not a strong visual learner. He was motivated to complete his book and was willing to take suggestions to do so. Exercising short-term visual memory will be helpful to him in school.

Visual Memory and the Episodic Lane

Since episodic memory is location oriented, the visual learner benefits greatly from a unique environment. These students will readily store visual information about the following:

- Field trips
- Bulletin boards
- Posters
- Colored paper
- Accessories
- Where you were standing when you shared information
- What you were wearing when you taught a lesson

Our brains automatically create maps of our surroundings. In the structure called the hippocampus, the environment is automatically mapped. Not only do brain cells called "place" cells create connections, but our genes are also affected. We are truly in charge of our students' environments, and as a result, we are changing their brains (Kosick, 2000)! Beyond that, it is the visual learners who will most easily recall the color of the carpet, the pictures on the wall, and what people are wearing. They may also store information that we do not deem important, but it may be very important to them.

I am teaching a self-contained fifth-grade class. It is time for social studies, and today I am giving a recall test. We have been covering U.S. government.

I see Isaac looking at me as I walk around the room. I move to my desk. He stares. I move to the front of the room by one of the computers. His eyes follow me. I am beginning to get uncomfortable. I have several teaching spots in my classroom. In fact, I try to be consistent in choosing a spot for a specific unit and sticking to it. I move to the social studies teaching spot. I pretend to be arranging some of the research materials. As I arrive at the mark, I look straight at Isaac. A smile suddenly crosses his face, and he frantically begins to write.

After the exam, the students have a short break. I walk over to Isaac and say, "Were you having some trouble on the exam?"

"Boy, was I, Mrs. Sprenger! But the minute you went to that spot by the maps and the flag, it all started coming back to me. I could see you pointing out the parts of the flag and explaining what they stood for. Then I could picture the notes I had taken. You walked over there just in time. I was afraid I wouldn't finish."

Figure 4.1

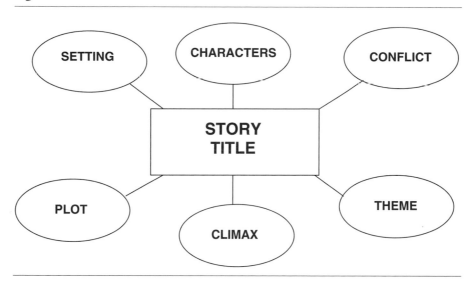

Not all students rely this heavily on episodic memory, but some really capture information this way. The stronger visual learner can store a great deal of material through this memory lane. These students have what Armstrong (1994) calls spatial intelligence and have the ability to graphically characterize ideas.

If this area is a strength:

- Ask these students to help "accessorize" the room for the topic.
- Allow these students to create visuals, such as charts, graphs, and maps.
- Help students create memory journals in which they can design ideal learning environments.

If visual episodic memory is a weakness:

- Give extra time for copying from the chalkboard or overhead.
- Use well-organized handouts with extra "white space" to prevent the student from becoming overwhelmed with visual stimuli.
- While the strong visual learner creates the atmosphere, the weaker student can create a guided tour of the new location. This will give her the opportunity to scrutinize the episodic material.

Episodic memory relates to stories, especially autobiographical data. Students can often tell their own stories, but may have difficulty organizing episodes in which they are not personally involved. It may be helpful to use story maps or story organizers. (See Figure 4.1.)

Visual Memory and the Procedural Lane

Micayla is in my second-grade class. We have recently begun to learn about subtracting two-digit numbers. Today, as she has for the last three days, Micayla raises her hand and asks to go to the restroom just as we are about to start the subtraction process on the board. I reluctantly let her leave the room. She is gone for the entire group lesson.

I check her homework paper and see that she just isn't getting the process. I decide to keep her in at recess to ask her a few questions.

"Micayla, are you feeling okay? I've noticed that you are using the restroom more often."

"Mrs. Sprenger, every time you start subtracting, my head spins and my stomach hurts! I just have to leave the room."

"Maybe your stomach hurts because you are having trouble understanding the subtraction."

"I know I'm having trouble understanding. There are just too many things to do. I just won't use subtraction when I grow up," she says knowingly.

"Do you think if we go through this one step at a time that you might be able to understand it?" I suggest.

"I try to listen when you give the steps, but by the time you say the second thing to do, I've forgotten the first thing!"

Micayla was having trouble sequencing through visual memory. I was showing the students how to do the problems as I proceeded step by step. Instead of just being told and shown the problem-solving procedure, Micayla needed to have written instruction that she could refer back to. Here's an example of the type of instruction I mean:

- Begin by placing one number above the other so the tens-place digits and ones-place digits are lined up. Draw a line under the bottom number.

$$\frac{\begin{array}{r}67\\45\end{array}}{}$$

- Subtract the two digits in the ones place $(7 - 5 = 2)$.

$$\begin{array}{r} 67 \\ \underline{45} \\ 2 \end{array}$$

- Subtract the digits in the tens-place column $(6 - 4 = 2)$ and place the answer below the line to the left of the other number below the line.

$$\begin{array}{r} 67 \\ \underline{45} \\ 22 \end{array}$$

This implicit memory system is quite important in our school day. There are many procedures that students must be aware of. Dr. Mel Levine (2002) divides procedural memory into two types: motor procedural memory and nonmotor procedural memory. The visual learner likes to learn these procedures by seeing them, either in print or in pictures or diagrams. For motor procedural memory, watching the procedure may be sufficient for some learners, but for others to get the sequence, it must be written.

I have always wanted to learn to juggle. My son can juggle. My brother can juggle. My best friend can juggle. Each one of them has tried to teach me to juggle. They have taken me through the process step by step.

"Just watch, Mom," my son would say. "First you toss this in the air like this. Are you watching?"

I'm sure my eyes would just glaze over. I am definitely a visual-auditory-kinesthetic learner. I'm not good at doing things with my hands. I give up.

In the summer of 1993, I awaken to sunshine pouring through the window. I have no workshops today. The kids are busy. The house is clean. What am I going to do with my day?

For whatever reason, juggling pops into my head. Today, I'm going to learn how to juggle! But how? I can go to the bookstore at the mall and get that book, *Juggling for the Complete Klutz!* I'm a visual learner. If I read about it, I bet I can do it.

I dress and go to the mall and get the book. Then I head straight home, anxious to see if this is going to work. I read the first section of the book. It takes me about ten minutes. I look at the steps. I read Step 1 and try it. Practice, I tell myself. I practice the step until I have it down pretty well. Then I go to the next step. In short, within an hour, I am juggling! Oh, you won't see me in the circus, but I can keep three apples in the air for ten seconds—which can seem like a really long time! Try it.

Educators must be aware of this type of need in the visual learner. In math class, which is full of procedures, each step should be written out. Simply showing it may not be enough to reach all students.

Examine the strategies for teaching the following story problem:

Mrs. Green's fourth-grade class had 20 students at the beginning of the year. Before Thanksgiving, three students moved away. By May, five new students had joined the class. How many students are now in Mrs. Green's class?

Drawing a picture of the problem is helpful for most visual learners. (See Figure 4.2.)

In addition to the picture, step-by-step instructions would assist learners like me:

Step 1: Write the number of students at the beginning of the year.

20

Step 2: Subtract three students from that number.

$20 - 3 = \underline{}$

Step 3: Add 5 students to the answer in Step 2. $(20 - 3 = 17)$

$17 + 5 = 22$

Step 4: The final answer is 22.

Procedures are used in most content areas. Our students are asked to remember how to

- Write a letter in proper form
- Use punctuation marks in correct places
- Diagram sentences
- Follow procedure in lab experiments
- Use capitalization properly

Figure 4.2

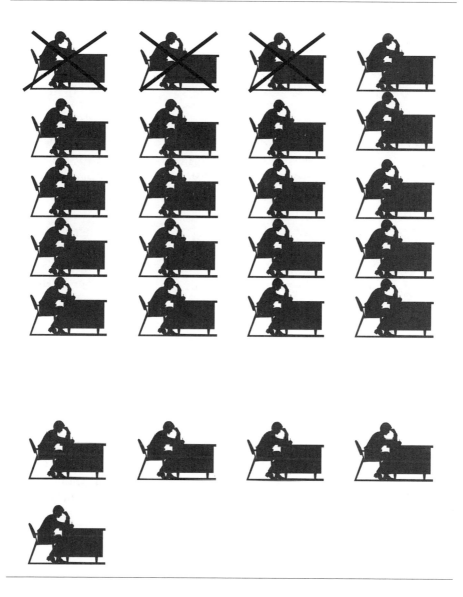

For students to place a procedure in long-term memory, they will need to see how it is done, as well as read how it is done. For the nonmotor procedures, like lab experiments, post the step-by-step instructions. The format for letter writing can also be made available on a poster or bulletin board.

Visual Memory and Conditioned Response

To emphasize how we use different parts of our brains, I used to give my sixth-grade students the following challenge: "Anyone who can tell me the months of the year in alphabetical order in less than thirty seconds gets to pick the song for the next break."

Usually the students are whipping out notebook paper and pencil, and frantically trying to create the solution. It is always interesting to see the process. Some students write the months of the year in order and begin numbering them alphabetically. Others sit and repeat the months and quickly try to write them in alphabetical order.

What was surprising to me was that some of my students did nothing. No attempt at the task was made. When I asked these students why they were not participating, I received one of two answers: "That's not enough time. I'm just not quick enough." Or "I don't know all the months."

The first response made me feel guilty. I should not have been putting time restraints on them. Even though this was for fun, some kids can't deal with the pressure. So they give up. It makes me wonder how many give up on standardized tests when they hear what the time limits are! The second response made me sad. Some of these sixth-grade students didn't know the months. The automaticity hadn't set in for them. This skill would not be needed as much as others, but this was an indication that students need more work on these conditioned response memories.

Instant access to information becomes a must as students progress through school. This includes letter formation, spelling, simple arithmetic, multiplication tables, and skip counting. If automaticity is not reached in these and other areas, students can easily lag behind.

One strategy for this memory lane is the use of flash cards. The visual learner will especially benefit from them. Vocabulary words can be written on one side with the definition on the other. A picture, if available, may also be helpful.

Metaphors are often remembered by the visual learner. Students can create the metaphor and add an illustration to reinforce the concept. I often had my students make mobiles using hangers. The metaphor was placed within the body of the hanger and the details hung from it.

Figure 4.3

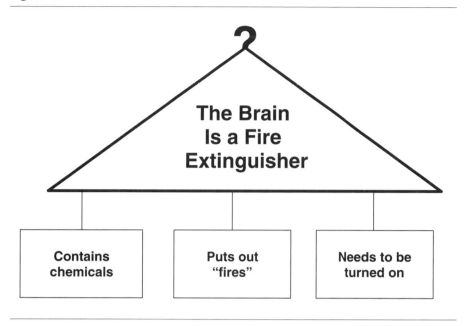

Rhythm and rhyme are excellent for this memory lane. For the visual learners, I found that having them write the song or poem in their own handwriting and repeatedly practicing placed the information into long-term memory. For some, pictures to go with the song or poem were necessary.

Visual Memory and Emotions

Research suggests that emotions are a very powerful aspect of learning. According to Joseph LeDoux, when the emotional system is activated, so are other learning systems in the brain. One may be doing some problem solving, but without emotional activation, the intensity is less, as is arousal. Fewer areas of the brain are involved in the learning. In some studies, emotions have been found to amplify explicit memories. This is due to a release of chemicals that influence the amygdala (the emotional center) and the hippocampus (the factual center) (LeDoux, 2002).

Tobias arrives early one morning. I see him waiting for the bus to drop off his friends. It is a brisk day and I need to get into my classroom and put up a new bulletin board. I smile and say, "Good morning," as I rush past him. He nods, but there is no other response. This reaction is unusual. I stop as I reach the door.

"Tobias, could you come to my room and help me?" I ask.

Again, he nods. He follows me into the building, down the hall, and into my classroom in silence.

"I'm putting up a new bulletin board today. I'd like to get it up before first hour. Do you mind helping me?"

Again, he nods.

"You seem very quiet this morning. Are you awake yet?" I say this only half joking. This adolescent, like so many others, is often sleep-deprived.

"I guess so," is his brief answer.

I take out the posters that I need for my unit on *Romeo and Juliet*. As I unroll them, I hand them to Tobias. He takes the first one, a drawing of Shakespeare, and staples it to the board for me. The second poster is Romeo looking up at Juliet on the balcony. Again, he staples. Then I hand him a fighting scene. Tobias stops and looks at it.

"Is this the play that's supposed to be like that movie *West Side . . .* something?" he asks.

"*West Side Story* has a similar theme. I take it that you've seen the movie?"

"My mom made me watch it over the summer. I hated that stupid singing. Some of the fighting was okay."

I watched as his eyes started to light up. As we continued to complete the bulletin board, Tobias began telling me the entire *West Side Story* plot—from beginning to end. The Shakespearian scene on the bulletin board triggered some emotional memories of the movie and the details came spilling out.

Emotional memories are powerful and will be retrieved more readily in an emotional state similar to the one in which the memory was made. According to Andreasen (2001), "The amygdala may work primarily to integrate memories learned from different modalities and memories with strong emotional valence." The visual learner will access this emotional state through pictures or words. To add emotional visual memory to lessons, there are a variety of possibilities:

- Video clips
- Posters
- Scrapbooks made by the students
- Drawings of their feelings about the content
- Editorials with pictures or cartoons
- Poetry with pictures created by students or "mental videos" or pictures

Emotion can wipe out memories as well. It behooves us to be somewhat careful when we are adding emotional components to our teaching. Dr. David Diamond observed rats as they first learned to find a platform in a water maze and then promptly forgot what they had just learned when a cat appeared. The fear caused them to focus on the cat and forget the learning (Hayes, 2002).

VISUAL MEMORY: I'LL SHOW YOU WHAT I KNOW!

Thus far, we have focused on instructional strategies for the visual learner. Another way to differentiate for this learner is to provide choices of products.

One must be very specific, using a rubric with the criteria that will be assessed. Students must be made aware that the product must reflect the knowledge and understanding that has been gained.

Some of the possible product choices for visual memory would be a/an

- Scrapbook
- Brochure
- Video
- Poster
- Collage
- Editorial
- Short story
- Essay
- Comic book

Figure 4.4

	1	2	3	4	
Organization	No sequence to presentation; cannot understand	Difficulty understanding; Presenter jumps around	Logical sequence; audience can follow	Logical & interesting sequence; easy to follow	
Content	Presenter does not understand information; cannot answer questions	Presenter can only answer simple questions; uncomfortable with material	At ease with content, but little elaboration	Presenter knows content well, elaborates & explains well	
Creativity	No creativity or imagination used; single source	No creativity or imagination used; more than one source	Creative and imaginative; more than one source	Well integrated information in a creative and imaginative manner	
Mechanics	Four or more spelling and/or grammatical errors	Three or more spelling and/or grammatical errors	Two or more spelling and/or grammatical errors	No spelling and/or grammatical errors	
Delivery	Presenter mumbles and is difficult to hear and understand	Presenter mispronounces words and is difficult to hear	Clear voice; pronounces most words correctly	Clear voice; all words pronounced and used correctly	

If the product will be presented to the class, the presentation may be assessed by the class as well as the teacher. Be sure to include what you want to assess in the rubric. The students may be helpful in this process.

BLOOM'S TAXONOMY AND THE VISUAL LEARNER

Bloom's taxonomy for the cognitive domain is used by many school districts. Our desire to help our students reach higher level thinking can be guided by this structure. In identifying intellectual outcomes, the domain is divided into several levels (Bloom, 1956).

Beginning with the least complicated and moving toward the most complicated, the levels are as follows:

- *Knowledge:* recalling facts, terms, definitions, and basic concepts

- *Comprehension:* organizing, comparing, translating, interpreting, giving descriptions, and stating main ideas to demonstrate understanding

- *Application:* applying acquired knowledge, facts, techniques, and rules in a way to solve problems

- *Analysis:* breaking information into its parts by identifying motives or causes; making inferences and finding evidence to support generalizations. Categorization is one way to reorganize information to show analysis.

- *Synthesis:* compiling information together in a different way by uniting elements in a new pattern or suggesting alternative solutions

- *Evaluation:* based on a set of criteria, presenting and defending opinions by making judgments about information, legitimacy of ideas, or quality of work

To encourage critical thinking in the visual learner, there are several questions that may be employed at each level. Keep in mind that these are only suggestions. Your content area, level of processing, and teaching style may influence the types of questions you use. Students may show you what they know by choosing a product to answer questions requiring the attainment of certain levels of thinking.

Knowledge

Words to use include:

Omit	Define	Name
Where	Label	Relate
Which	Show	Tell
Choose	Spell	Recall
Find	List	Select
How	Match	

Some possible questions include:

How would you describe . . . ?

How would you show . . . ?

Can you select . . . ?

Match the items . . .

Label the parts of . . .

Comprehension

Words to use for this level include:

Compare	Extend	Rephrase
Contrast	Illustrate	Translate
Demonstrate	Infer	Summarize
Interpret	Outline	Show
Explain	Relate	Classify

Some possible questions include:

Illustrate . . .

How would you show . . . ?

Classify the items . . .

Outline the chapter . . .

Using a Venn diagram, compare and contrast . . .

Application

Words to use for this level include:

Apply	Interview	Select
Build	Make use of	Solve
Choose	Organize	Utilize
Construct	Experiment with	Model
Develop	Plan	Identify

Some possible questions include:

How would you organize . . . ?

How would you show your understanding of . . . ?

What facts would you select to show . . . ?

How would you apply what you learned in order to develop a . . . ?

Analysis

Words to use for this level include:

Analyze	Examine	Theme
Categorize	Inspect	Relationships
Classify	Simplify	Function
Compare	Survey	Motive
Contrast	Take part in	Inference
Discover	Test for	Assumption
Dissect	Distinguish	Conclusion
Divide	List	

Some possible questions include:

Show how _____ is related to_____.

Identify the differences between . . .

Simplify the _____ by using a graphic that will distinguish . . .

Examine the reasons for _____ and categorize their usefulness.

Can you identify the different parts of . . . ?

Synthesis

Words to use for this level include:

Build	Imagine	Change
Choose	Invent	Adapt
Combine	Make up	Minimize
Compile	Originate	Maximize
Compose	Plan	Delete
Construct	Predict	Theorize
Create	Propose	Elaborate
Design	Solve	Test
Develop	Suppose	Improve
Estimate	Discuss	Happen
Formulate	Modify	Change

Some possible questions include:

Modify the current plan to include . . .

Design a model that would . . .

Create a better model of . . .

What could be done to maximize . . . ?

Compose a better ending for . . .

Evaluation

Words to use for this level include:

Award	Measure	Support
Choose	Compare	Prove
Conclude	Mark	Disprove
Criticize	Rate	Assess
Decide	Recommend	Influence
Defend	Select	Perceive
Determine	Agree	Value
Dispute	Interpret	Estimate
Evaluate	Explain	Influence
Judge	Appraise	Deduct
Justify	Prioritize	

Some possible questions include:

What would you cite to defend the actions of . . . ?

How would you prioritize . . . ?

Why would you select . . . ?

What truths or fallacies can you show . . . ?

What information would you use to justify . . . ?

Given the following data, what conclusion would you draw . . . ?

A Note About Synthesis

Synthesizing information is something that is done in working memory on a regular basis. When our students are attending to us, they are taking our words, recoding them, attaching them to previously stored information, and making meaning (Levine, 2002). Let's give them credit where it is due. Bring their attention to what their brains are capable of doing and share with them that they are performing higher-order thinking skills. This may be just the boost of confidence they need.

DIFFERENT STROKES

1. Both visual and nonvisual learners may benefit from an activity such as this: Put students in groups of three. Give the first student a picture to study for three minutes. Then ask the student to put the picture away and explain to the second student, in detail, what the picture looked like. Student Number 2 listens carefully and writes down what he or she has heard. Student 2 gives the description to Student 3 who tries to draw the picture. Give students time for discussion and reflection. If time is available, repeat the process with different pictures and offer the opportunity for students to switch roles.

2. Oprah Lemonfry! I had to name this activity after this special name one of my students gave his lemon! To aid with observation and descriptive writing, I bring lemons to school. Each student is given a lemon, told to give the lemon a name, and then write a description of the lemon. The students are not to write their names on their papers. After the description is written, the lemons are collected. The descriptions are collected and passed out randomly. The students read the descriptions and are then asked to find the lemon that matches the description. This is an excellent way for students to see how important detail can be. The final step in the activity is to collect the lemons, place them all on a table, and see if the original owners can find their lemons. (There are sometimes incidents of students taking the incorrect lemon and shouts of "lemon-napping" are heard.)

Differentiation Design

5

Remembering Auditory Information

Janice comes into my room before school. She throws a stack of papers on my desk as she shakes her head.

"Good morning to you, too!" I say good-naturedly as I glance at the papers.

"Okay, good morning," Janice replies half-heartedly. "This is driving me crazy. I write the assignment on the board every day. The kids know that they are to look at the homework spot every day and write down the assignment. Usually I have the opportunity to direct their attention to the assignment, but once in awhile I run out of time . . ."

" . . . and you have students who either aren't doing their homework or who are not following directions," I finish her sentence for her.

"Yes! Now how many times do I have to go over this procedure with them?"

"You said a key word, Jan," I reply. "Procedure. It's not in procedural memory yet, and my guess would be that your auditory learners walk out of your room without even seeing the assignment. Let's go ask Margo about this; I think she has some resources."

At that moment Margo sticks her head in the door to say hello. She sees the expression on Janice's face. "Would I be intruding if I come in?" she asks.

Janice explains her concerns and Margo suggests she take a closer look at the students and their papers.

"So, if I look at the papers that are incorrect, I should see my auditory learners?"

"Very likely, but we have to take into consideration the fact that any child can mess up an assignment!" Margo suggests. "Let's go through some of these papers and look at the names of the students whose papers are missing and try to determine if you need to beef up some auditory communication and reinforce some procedures in your classroom."

We sit down and check out the students whose papers are missing. There are only two. "Tell us about Clarice. Does she talk a lot? Does she give you eye contact? If you don't give her a chance to talk about her learning, does she lose it?" Margo asks.

"You hit the nail on the head with her," Janice responds, "but that doesn't fit Doug, and his paper is missing, too."

"I've seen Doug in the hall quite often for the last few years. I've nicknamed him the 'Hall Monitor.' What is he doing to get sent out of class?" I inquire.

"He can't sit still. He's always bugging someone. He rocks in his chair. He has to be kinesthetic," Janice declares.

"If he's kinesthetic–auditory, he isn't seeing the assignment on the board either," Margo shares.

"Okay, if I make time to verbally direct them to the assignment, will that be good enough, or should I always read it to them?" Janice asks resignedly.

"Direct them to the assignment and have *them* read it aloud. That will be even better," Margo suggests.

Even with the best intentions, we often overlook important methods when dealing with different learning strengths. The auditory/verbal learner has the strength of learning through listening and speaking (Grinder, 1991; Rose & Nicholl, 1997; Tileston, 2000). Such learners store information in the different memory lanes in an auditory fashion.

Many times these learners do not excel in a school setting because they are not interested in putting their knowledge into print. Written book reports can be a real chore. Reading the book often can be a difficult task. Oral book reports are more satisfying to this learner, and I frequently find that this student can share an enormous amount of information verbally. Written reports, on the other hand, are often short with few details.

DO YOU TEACH FOR AUDITORY MEMORY?

It is easy to think that when we are disseminating information (sometimes called lecturing) that we are meeting the needs of the auditory learner. This is true only if we speak in small chunks of information and allow the students to discuss for short periods in between the chunks.

If you yourself are an auditory learner and have strong auditory memory, you may answer many of the following questions affirmatively:

1. Do I do a lot of lecturing?

2. Do I easily get off track when I am speaking (go off on tangents)?

3. Do I use my voice in my teaching (change volume, tone, etc.)?

4. Am I easily distracted by sounds? (Do kids tapping, clicking their pens, or talking get on my nerves?)

5. Do I rely on verbal information and expect it from my students?

6. Do I talk to myself often?

7. Do I recognize student comments by paraphrasing them?

8. Do I give "sermons" in response to misbehavior?

9. Do I rarely use visual aids?

10. Do I often have students read aloud, or do I find myself reading aloud to them?

If you answer "yes" to many of these questions, you may have an auditory preference. Examine your practices carefully. Lecture and discussion may work for you and your auditory learners, but you may be losing many of your other students. If you are especially aware of a preference for lecture without discussion, you are also losing the auditory learners in your class.

DIFFERENTIATION DESIGN FOR LEARNERS WITH STRONG AUDITORY MEMORY

Those with strong auditory memories will often appear inattentive. They don't need to get or give eye contact. Instead they may cock their heads in order to have their ear closer to the speaker. They may resent it if you insist that they take notes or write down homework assignments or procedures.

If you are an auditory teacher, you may understand this and not even notice that some students are gazing out the window. As an auditory teacher, you may be able to use your voice to gain attention and make specific points. That will be engaging to many of your students, and the strong auditory learners will benefit most.

In past years, it was thought that the auditory–kinesthetic learner caused the most trouble in school and often would drop out. Recently, though, this thought has changed. Perhaps our classrooms are nontraditional enough with discussions and group work to provide for many of the needs of these learners. Or perhaps it was never really those learners who were in jeopardy, but rather that the kinesthetic learner with a strong auditory second preference was labeled auditory rather than kinesthetic. The talking in class may have been more disruptive than the movement. Regardless of theories, statistics, or models, our classrooms must honor the learner who remembers best by listening and speaking.

Auditory Memory and the Semantic Lane

Storing semantic information for the student with auditory strengths can be both challenging and simple. The short-term memory process allows us a bit more time with sounds. In other words, a picture, graph, or slide may disappear from immediate memory in milliseconds, but the act of repeating words and sounds allows us to hold onto auditory information longer. Those with less auditory inclination can benefit by training themselves to repeat information until they can either write it down or create a visual for it. The strong auditory learner automatically does the repetition. He or she can often then "carry" it into working memory and attempt to make connections for lasting memory. Those of us who are stronger visually may need to "see" the information during the working memory process.

The semantic strategies for auditory learners may be attractive to many types of learners. In their book, *Making Connections: Teaching and the Human Brain* (1994), Geoffrey and Renate Caine say, "As we talk about a subject or skill in complex and appropriate ways—and that includes making jokes and playing games—we actually begin to feel better about the subject and master it" (p. 131). As we offer strategies to our students, we must keep in mind that differentiation involves finding both a comfort and a challenge level for learning. Those strategies might include combinations of the following:

1. Small-group discussion

2. Debate

3. Books on tape

4. Interviews

5. Oral reports

6. Mnemonics involving rhythm and rhyme

7. Conferencing

8. Radio talk shows

9. Large-group discussion

10. Oral interpretation

Auditory learners need to hear themselves (Marshall, 2001). Keep in mind that knowledge may not be real to this learner until he has talked about it!

It is late Thursday afternoon. The building is empty except for five of us in the library who are working on the School Improvement Plan. This is an ongoing process, but there always seem to be "crunch" times when we spend more time working on the plan.

A man appears at the door. "When do I get my wife back?" Tony, Janice's husband, is addressing the group. "I need her to continue filling me in on your differentiation process. I'm having a heck of a time this year!"

Tony teaches at the high school level. This year he has two beginning Spanish classes and three Senior English classes. One of the English classes is Advanced Placement.

Margo smiles and says, "I didn't think you high school teachers ever needed any help. I thought you knew everything!"

I quickly come to the defense of secondary teachers. "Hey, now. Watch it! When I was teaching high school, I had more questions and just as many problems with kids as we do here. Sometimes I think the bigger the student, the bigger the problems!"

We look at the clock and realize that it is time to wrap up the meeting. Tony and Janice help me carry materials into the principal's office.

"I'm really interested in brain research and differentiation," Tony begins. "Adolescents are difficult to deal with. I don't know if it's hormones or what, but they act like they understand and then they really don't. I gave all my classes the learning style test that you gave Janice. It was pretty amazing. I think I'm an auditory learner, so I teach that way a lot. Probably too much. The most interesting thing I learned from this is that the kids in my classes who are strong auditory learners are not happy with my lectures. I didn't realize they needed to talk. The visual learners are always busy taking copious notes. The kinesthetic learners are probably asleep or in trouble because I don't let them move, and the strong auditory learners cause trouble because they need to speak and will speak out impulsively. It's like they just have to say something or they'll burst! I thought at first that I was dealing with several attention deficit students with all this impulsive talking, but from Janice I found out that if they don't get to speak, they'll stay pretty stuck on the information they need to talk about and I lose them for the rest of the lecture!"

"You care enough to examine your methods and your students' learning preferences. With just this information, you can make a big difference in the success of your students," I reply, sincerely impressed.

"Do you think it would be possible for me to spend a day here and watch the strategies that you, Margo, and my wife use for differentiation?" Tony asks.

"I think that would be a great idea. I often observe in the primary grades. Those teachers know how to keep kids moving and under control. I have borrowed many of their strategies. I think we all would be happy to share!"

Auditory Memory and the Episodic Lane

One might think that this lane would be difficult for the student with a strong auditory preference. After all, episodic memory seems to be so visual. I asked some strong auditory learners about this and an interesting conversation ensued.

I asked John, a colleague and contemporary of mine, where he was when he heard about JFK's assassination. He smiled. His eyes moved back and forth. "I was in school. It was my sophomore year in high school. History class. I remember Mr. Pope's words. "Kids, this is a very sad day, one that your children will read about in their history books. Today our president was shot."

"Wow, John! I was in English class. I don't think Miss Feasel said anything. I just remember staring at the P.A. system speaker. Someone said the president had been shot. And later he said killed. I remembered the English classroom to get the information. Did you picture your history class?"

"No, the words, Marilee, just the words. They're my memory."

I realized that episodic memory is especially powerful when it becomes an "event." And even with this information, I had to adapt to the idea that an event can be more verbal than visual to some people. The question became, How do I create an episode that is unique for the auditory learner? Here are some suggestions.

If this area is a strength:

1. Take students on field trips involving group work and discussion.

2. Play music in the classroom.

3. Have this learner lead a "tour" of the room, discussing each poster, picture, graph, and so forth.

4. Make use of guest speakers whenever possible, making them aware of the need for verbal interaction with the students.

5. Word walls, as described in *The Word Wall, Teaching Vocabulary Through Immersion* (Green, 1993), may be an important part of your classroom literacy. Those with strong auditory memory may need and want to review and recite these words.

If this area is a weakness:

1. Encourage students to repeat directions aloud or to themselves.

2. When using music with lyrics for episodic memory, write out the lyrics that are meaningful and memorable.

3. Promote oral summaries of field trips and assemblies.

Episodic memories that truly become events in our students' lives form strong memories. In the book, *A Good Start in Life*, the authors state that for children, "being able to remember events they experienced in the past is a basis for forming ideas about the world and about themselves"

(Herschkowitz & Herschkowitz, 2002, p.188). To promote oral tradition and verbal discussion, talk about the history of the world and how information was handed down from generation to generation. The auditory learner may use a brief "map" of the story, while other learners may benefit from verbalizing the stories while using mind maps and story maps.

Auditory Memory and the Procedural Lane

Lemar is in eighth grade when he becomes part of my geography class. He lives with a foster family as his father is in jail and his mother left when he was quite young. He has four foster siblings who all come from similar backgrounds. I am pleased with Lemar's communication abilities. He finds his niche with a group of students, answers lower-level questions in class, and appears interested in the subject matter.

It is the end of a unit on the states. The room is set up in modality centers. That is, there is a center for creating visual products about some states, a center for kinesthetic activities such as role play, and a center for verbal projects such as cassette players and musical selections for background to oral presentations.

I find Lemar moving from center to center. As the other students are engaged in their projects, he starts a poster at the visual center and seems to change his mind. He then goes to the kinesthetic center and joins some students in the creation of a dance to explain some of the history of Hawaii. After a few minutes, he leaves the dance and wanders to the auditory center. He is looking over his options when I approach.

"Having trouble deciding what you want to do?" I ask.

"Yeah. These things are dumb," he replies.

This response surprises me. My first reaction is to get angry. After all the work I put into offering these students choices, I did not like to hear that they were "dumb."

"I saw you get involved in the dance. Don't you like to dance?" I inquire.

"Those kids kept telling me what to do. I would just get one thing figured out and think I was done, and they'd get mad and tell me to start over and add the next step. They were making me feel stupid. This whole thing is dumb."

The light bulb went on. Lemar is a child of poverty. According to the work of Ruby Payne (1998), many students from generational poverty are kinesthetic learners as touch is an important part of their communication system. That made sense, since he was attracted to the kinesthetic area. These students are also deficient in procedural memory. That is, they have trouble with completion of a multistep process. This may be due to a lack of modeling at home and the lack of procedural self-talk that takes us step by step through processes.

"Of the options at the three centers, which would you find least 'dumb?'" I ask.

Lemar looks around and thinks for a minute. "I guess I'd want to tape an interview," he replies.

I take Lemar to the auditory center and pull out the directions for taping an expert interview. "First, you need to come up with the list of questions. Why don't you do that now, and then we'll figure out what comes next," I suggest.

Lemar nods, takes out some materials, and starts writing.

I was surprised that he didn't go back to the kinesthetic activities, but perhaps playing with that cassette recorder and microphone was more appealing. When he finished his questions, I took him to the next step. This was a five-step procedure, and he wasn't used to keeping so many things in mind. Even though the instructions were written, reading them and holding them in his mind were not working for him. The difficulty with procedural auditory memory is exacerbated in students with poor reading abilities and whose preference is not that modality.

Procedural memory that relies on auditory sequencing can be difficult for many students. Working memory must hold the sequence long enough to make the connections and complete the task. The strong auditory learner resents having to read each step, while the student weak in this area requires support. In this area, knowing your students' strengths and pairing or grouping them can reduce stress. Let the student with strengths in auditory procedural memory guide the weaker students. The best "team leader" for nonmotor procedural processes is the one who can remember the steps, keep them straight, and verbalize them well to the other teammates. At the same time, the visual learner who likes to read can read the steps to the leader.

The student with strengths in this area may appear weak when it comes to written procedures. Reading is not something this individual wants to do. Procedures that are written on the board or posted visually in some form are easily ignored. It is best to draw attention to these, have the auditory learner read them aloud, or have her repeat them after they are read. For the "translators" that I mentioned in Chapter 2, reminding students that the assignment is on the board with ten seconds remaining of class may be frustrating for them and cause incorrect or incomplete assignments.

Muscle Memory. Motor procedural memory is not a problem for the student with strong auditory memory as long as the procedure is spoken and the student is asked and is able to repeat it. The key words here are *spoken* and *repeated*. It is this learner who usually does well playing Simon Sez. Listening to directions and following them in simple steps is quite easy for this type of learner.

Whether the auditory student's second preference is visual or kinesthetic will make a difference with this motor procedural memory. If movement comes easily, following verbal directions and moving accordingly will be easier and stored more quickly. If this learner has more difficulty with movement and "hands-on" activities, the process is a bit more tedious. She may have to visualize those verbal instructions to "get a picture" of what she is to do. For this learner, the physical movement is somewhat delayed and takes longer to get into long-term memory.

Auditory Memory and Conditioned Response

It seems that all of our students enjoy music. The student with strong auditory memory may have a very strong preference and even display musical talent. These learners have thousands of song lyrics, melodies, and even artists stored in long-term memory. Consequently, using music is an easy and powerful way for them to store information.

Because these learners are compelled to answer rhetorical questions, believing they have to have the "last word," it is usually simply a matter of some oral repetition to get information into this memory lane.

Conditioned response activities might include

- Oral quizzes
- Rehearsal through "quiz shows" like *Jeopardy*
- Poetry
- Singing information to familiar tunes
- Creating metaphors
- Using a tape recorder to record questions and answers (This learner stores information in this format quickly and easily.)

Figure 5.1   Rice Krispie Feats of Memory

Topic	Snap	Krackle	Pop
Nouns	Finger snapping for the *person*	"Crackling" fire for the *place*	Cork popping noise for the *thing*
Reducing fractions	"Snap" the numerator into its factors	"Crackle" (hiss) as you factor the denominator	"Pop" out the fraction that equals 1

- Using your voice—tone, pitch, volume—to emphasize certain words or definitions (These may serve as response triggers for this sensitive learner.)

We all sometimes feel like Pavlov's dog when we instantly respond to a stimulus. Those with a strong auditory preference can use those sounds as cues to learning. A teacher I met uses what she calls the "Rice Krispie" method: "Snap," "Krackle," and "Pop" information into memory using sounds that you can make with your mouth, hands, or feet (See Figure 5.1.) Once the students associate the learning with the sounds, work on transferring the learning to the semantic pathway. In other words, once the information is tied to the sounds, have the students practice putting the information on paper by repeating the sounds in their heads. (It can be disturbing if during an assessment students are making noises to jog their memories!)

The auditory learner has many strong capabilities if his active working memory is also keen. With these strengths, this student may be able to

- Pronounce or learn the meanings of new words
- Remember and follow directions easily
- Express himself easily due to fast word recall
- Speak in a very well thought-out manner
- Easily comprehend what is said

As a result, this may be the student leader when it comes to creating conditioned response activities. Information may be quickly remembered, organized, and inserted in metaphor, poem, joke, or song. Strong auditory learners often annoy visual teachers. They may be continuously asked to "quiet down." Offering this student the opportunity to create and perhaps lead this type of activity will provide an outlet for the speaking, along with making this learner a valuable asset to the class.

Emotions and the Auditory Learner

You can hear it in their voices. They may not be able to look you in the eye. They may not cock their heads in confusion. You may misread their body language as they express themselves. To pick up on the commitment to learning and information in the auditory learner, you must become adept at the tiny nuances that can be heard in their voices and sounds that they utter.

According to some research, there is a vast difference in the sounds that males and females make throughout the day. The average female is said to speak 7,000 to 8,000 words per day. She also utters about 4,000 sounds and makes 7,000 gestures. The average male speaks only 2,000 words per day, makes about 1,000 sounds, and gestures 3,000 times (Pease & Pease, 2000). Is it any wonder that as teachers we are constantly trying to get someone to be quiet?

With students who have a strong verbal preference, words will reveal their emotions and whether they have an emotional attachment to learning. These are the individuals in your classroom who will hang on your words long enough to determine your feelings. Will they hear excitement? Boredom? Frustration? Apathy?

As a visual teacher and learner, I often let my facial expressions reveal my feelings. One year, I had a very perceptive verbal learner in my classroom. Amos was rare in that he could control his "chatter" as long as he was able to talk during discussion. On one particular day, my daughter, Marnie, had called me during my lunch period to say that she was ill. She was away at college, and she complained of a fever along with a terrible headache and sore neck. I had visions of dangerous diseases—encephalitis or meningitis. Teaching at that moment was the last thing I wanted to do, but she was on her way to the clinic and I had a class to teach. Some research suggests that if we put a smile on our faces, positive responses will occur in the body. I needed something positive, so I faked a smile and walked into my classroom.

We were studying the brain. In fact, we were discussing the frontal lobes of the brain. As I was explaining that the frontal lobes are in charge of future planning and decision making, I started wondering if I had made the right decision in staying at school. Perhaps I should have jumped in the car and driven over to Marnie's campus. As my mind wandered, I made certain that the smile remained on my face and that I gave my students eye contact.

Amos rarely looked at me when I spoke. He could gaze out the window or lay his head on his book as he absorbed my words. When my mind started to wander, and I began worrying again about my daughter, Amos turned and looked at me. Although I was surprised to see him do this, I finished my presentation and gave the students a diagram of a brain to work on. Amos quietly worked for a few moments and then came up to my desk.

"Is everything okay, Mrs. Sprenger?" he asked with concern in his voice.

"Sure, Amos, can I help you with something?" I replied.

"Your voice sure changed while you were talking. Are you worried about something?" he continued.

I gave in and told him that I had been thinking about my daughter's illness. "I was trying hard not to show it," I admitted sheepishly.

"You didn't show it," Amos remarked. "I could hear it in your voice."

Learners who are sensitive to the sounds around them are difficult to fool. They also have a keen ear for minor changes in tonality, pitch, and volume. As I mentioned in Chapter 4, a bit of emotion can aid in memory storage, while emotional content that is too strong can prevent that same storage from occurring. For the student with a strong auditory preference, emotion can be added in the following ways:

- Music: these learners know more song lyrics than you do
- Debate: working with strong opinions that are backed up by solid research
- Role play: if the student is comfortable with any movement involved in the role play, voice can be used to create emotion
- Interviews: these can be with outsiders, or students can play the part of experts, participants, or onlookers for many situations
- Joke creating and telling
- Storytelling: most stories have an emotional component
- Playing an instrument

Concentration and the Auditory Learner

While it is often quite easy to keep the visual learner focused on visual content, the strong auditory learner may easily become distracted. Our voices frequently become "white noise" in a room full of auditory distractors. The student with strong auditory skills may also have a sensitivity to sounds. I had one student who would tell me at the end of class how many times the radiator turned on. There are also students who complain that other students are coughing, tapping their pens, or shuffling their feet! For this reason, I found that the following solutions were helpful:

- Seat the auditorily sensitive student away from obvious sounds, such as the radiator

- After sound interruptions, check in with this learner to return him to task
- Provide ear plugs or head phones to muffle sounds while the students are reading silently or working individually

I frequently think of auditory learners as "blind." They often don't see what others do. For instance, Amanda was an eighth grader on the basketball team who showed an auditory-kinesthetic-visual pattern. It was late March and uniforms needed to be turned in. I received a message to call Amanda's mother. She was informing me that Amanda could not find her uniform; she sounded frantic.

"Where is it supposed to be?" I asked calmly.

"Well, I washed it and thought I hung it in her closet, but Amanda says it's not there!" she replied.

"Have you looked in her closet?" I inquired.

"Well, no. But Amanda looked," was her response.

"Amanda is not a very visual person. My guess is that the uniform is where you put it. Will you look while I hold?"

"No problem. Portable phone. You're coming with me!" she quipped.

She reached the closet and I could hear hangers being moved. Suddenly I heard, "I can't believe it! It's right here. You were right, Mrs. Sprenger. And better yet, I don't think I'm crazy! I did put it where I thought I had."

We continued our conversation for a few minutes. I wanted to assure her that there was nothing wrong with Amanda. Her visual skills needed some honing, but lots of people in the world are exactly like her. They do very well.

AUDITORY MEMORY: I'LL TELL IT LIKE IT IS!

Giving the auditory learner choices when sharing new or old information can lead to interesting assessments. This student may want to express him- or herself through

- Song
- Speech
- Audiotape
- Poetry
- Oral test

- Group discussion
- Conference/Personal communication

For any oral presentation, be certain to use a rubric that covers the areas that prove that the student has met the criterion and your expectations.

As I have tried to emphasize, allowing the students to begin learning and sharing new information with their strengths gives them the confidence to then attempt other types of learning and assessment. Don't let this type of learner off the hook with only verbal assessment. It is important to be able to express knowledge in many ways. Our state standardized tests leave little room for oral defense. All of our students must be able to express knowledge in both written and oral formats.

BLOOM'S TAXONOMY AND THE AUDITORY LEARNER

The following list defines again each level of thinking in Bloom's (1956) taxonomy. The auditory learner should be encouraged to think at each of these levels.

- *Knowledge:* recalling facts, terms, definitions, and basic concepts

- *Comprehension:* organizing, comparing, translating, interpreting, giving descriptions, and stating main ideas to demonstrate understanding

- *Application:* applying acquired knowledge, facts, techniques, and rules in a way to solve problems

- *Analysis:* breaking information into its parts by identifying motives or causes; making inferences and finding evidence to support generalizations. Categorization is one way to reorganize information to show analysis.

- *Synthesis:* compiling information in a different way by uniting elements in a new pattern or suggesting alternative solutions.

- *Evaluation:* based on a set of criteria, presenting and defending opinions by making judgments about information, validity of ideas, or quality of work.

Students may tell you what they know through the use of different products that you feel are appropriate for the content.

Knowledge

Words to use for this level include:

Where	Label	Relate
Which	Show	Tell
Choose	Spell	Recall
Find	List	Select
How	Match	
Define	Name	

Some possible questions include:

How would you describe . . . ?

How would you say . . . ?

Can you relate . . . ?

Name the items . . .

Tell the parts of . . .

Comprehension

Words to use for this level include:

Compare	Infer	Summarize
Contrast	Outline	Show
Interpret	Relate	Classify
Explain	Rephrase	
Extend	Translate	

Some possible questions include:

Interpret . . .

How would you summarize . . . ?

Explain the items . . .

Interpret the chapter . . .

Create a dialogue in which two characters infer . . .

Application

Words to use for this level include:

Apply	Make use of	Solve
Choose	Organize	Utilize
Construct	Experiment with	Model
Develop	Plan	Identify
Interview	Select	

Some possible questions include:

How would you identify . . . ?

How would you explain your understanding of . . . ?

What facts would you select to tell . . . ?

How would you conduct an interview . . . ?

Analysis

Words to use for this level include:

Analyze	Examine	Theme
Categorize	Inspect	Relationships
Classify	Simplify	Function
Compare	Survey	Motive
Contrast	Take part in	Inference
Discover	Test for	Assumption
Dissect	Distinguish	Conclusion
Divide	List	

Some possible questions include:

Tell how _____ is related to_____.

Distinguish the differences between _____ and _____.

How could you classify the areas of . . . ?

Analyze the reasons for _____ and categorize their usefulness.

Can you compare the motives of each character?

Synthesis

Words to use for this level include:

Build	Imagine	Change
Choose	Invent	Adapt
Combine	Make up	Minimize
Compile	Originate	Maximize
Compose	Plan	Delete
Construct	Predict	Theorize
Create	Propose	Elaborate
Design	Solve	Test
Develop	Suppose	Improve
Estimate	Discuss	Happen
Formulate	Modify	Change

Some possible questions include:

Improve the current plan to include . . .

Imagine and explain a design that would . . .

Discuss the variables of a better model of . . .

What could be said to maximize the current concept or modify . . . ?

Compose a better ending to . . .

Evaluation

Words to use for this level include:

Award	Defend	Justify
Choose	Determine	Measure
Conclude	Dispute	Compare
Criticize	Evaluate	Mark
Decide	Judge	Rate

Recommend   Prioritize   Perceive

Select   Support   Value

Agree   Prove   Estimate

Interpret   Disprove   Deduct

Explain   Assess

Appraise   Influence

Some possible questions include:

What would you evaluate to defend the actions of . . . ?

How would you explain . . . ?

How would you interpret . . . ?

What information would you recommend to justify . . . ?

Given the following data, what conclusion would you draw?

DIFFERENT STROKES

1. Something as simple as the "telephone game" can be used to make learning fun and more meaningful for the auditory learner. Even high school students enjoy whispering secret information to others. Group the students in a circle and give each one a note card with a fact or part of a story written on it. The first student whispers the note card information to the next student. This student must repeat the new information and whatever is written on his own card. The last student relates the entire message. This can be done by rows as a competition to "hear" which group does the best job of relating credible information.

2. Auditory learners often talk to themselves. Most of us have our own internal dialogue that we use to help us understand what we are doing. Have all students explain to themselves—internally or by just moving their mouths—information that they have just received through lecture, reading, and so forth. Then ask students to find a partner and take turns explaining the material. This calls for the higher-level thinking skills of evaluation and synthesis.

Differentiation Design

6

Remembering by Doing

It's Thursday afternoon. We are using the gym as our classroom. We are studying Shakespeare. It's one of those interdisciplinary units that we don't know is an interdisciplinary unit. What we know is that there are several kinesthetic boys in our seventh-grade classrooms that cannot sit still who can run around the gym sword fighting until they get that need to move satisfied and sit down with the rest of the class to read and discuss the play.

I look up as David, Ryan, Doug, and Mick put down their "swords" and sit with the rest of us. We are choosing parts. Mick declares, "I want to be Romeo!"

Ryan objects, "I think Romeo should be taller. I'm taller than Mick. It should be me."

I am totally amazed to see these students arguing over a part in a Shakespearian play. Until I figured out how to keep them moving, they never participated in anything productive.

I look up at the doorway and see Janice looking in. I motion for her to enter and join us.

"What's going on here?" she asks David and Doug.

"We're gonna put on a play," Doug announces. "I'll get a big part. I get to sword fight in it, too. Probably get to kill someone."

The bell rings and the 32 students leave for their next class.

"Those boys seemed really excited. I don't know how you can handle all the noise and the moving around. Do you think you'll really get these kids to put on a play?" Janice asks.

"It's because I can handle the noise and I let those boys move around that we'll be able to put on the play. This class is seventy-five percent kinesthetic! If they don't move, no learning takes place at all. It's really much less stressful for me and the students to run the class this way . . . these students are really bright and talented. Now they'll have the chance to prove it!"

"If I decide to put on a play, will you help me? I've never done anything like this before. All we do is read the plays in the textbook and once in awhile act out a scene," Janice shares.

"That's a great start. Keep adding to the number of scenes that you perform. Soon you'll be ready for the whole thing. Why don't you help with the final performances when my students' parents come? That'll give you more experience!" I suggest.

She looks at me like she's just been tricked, but she's a good sport and nods.

Without a doubt, teaching to students who are kinesthetic learners is a challenge. Most of us have never been trained to teach to learners who need to move, touch, and try. They really go against the educational system as many of us know it. Students are supposed to sit quietly and listen, right?

DO YOU TEACH FOR KINESTHETIC MEMORY?

Let's quickly make a distinction between kinesthetic and procedural memory. Procedural memory involves repeating a task until it becomes second nature. Putting on makeup is an example of this. There is a specific order to applying makeup appropriately. The first few times one does it, it may take some thought. Does the liquid foundation go first and then the powder, or is it vice versa? Once the sequencing is repeated enough, however, there is little thought to the process.

Kinesthetic learning requires touch, movement, or sometimes an emotional response. Kinesthetic memory may at times be related to the emotional memory lane. For learners whose preference is kinesthetic, the trigger for the memory may involve manipulating an object, tapping a pencil, or moving around in their seats. Take another look at your teaching style. If you have strong kinesthetic memory, you may have teaching strategies that would cause you to answer the following questions with a resounding "Yes!":

1. Do I provide many hands-on activities?

2. Is movement something my body needs in the classroom?

3. Am I easily distracted by noise?

4. Do I often give affirming touches?

5. Do I usually have my students working on projects?

6. Am I comfortable using play dough, Koosh balls, or stuffed animals to provide tactile stimulation?

7. Am I comfortable providing frequent breaks and allowing movement?

8. Do I speak slowly?

9. Do I remember feelings and actions more easily than names and faces?

If you answered many of these questions affirmatively, you may have strong preferences for kinesthetic learning and memory. Think about the instructional strategies that you commonly use. Although the movement you provide will satisfy the learner with strong kinesthetic memory, it may cause stress for some of your other learners. Going back to Markova's (1992) work, a student with the VAK pattern, as an example, may be uncomfortable with hands-on activities. For this learner, the movement may be optional until she is ready to stretch from her more comfortable modality.

DIFFERENTIATION DESIGN FOR LEARNERS WITH STRONG KINESTHETIC MEMORY

Students with this learning preference may fidget, move around, and find something or someone to touch (Jones, 2002). This can cause many class disruptions as other students react to the activity. Providing an outlet for this learner's needs can change the atmosphere of the classroom, as well as provide more time for learning since "discipline" will be needed less.

Katie and Nick are walking around in the back of the room. I am doing a lesson on the Civil War. Some of the students are watching me as I walk from map to blackboard, trying to make connections in their brains. I throw out a few questions to see if the material is making sense to them. Both Nick and Katie have their hands raised. I call on Nick and he gives me the correct answer. They both continue their pacing.

Adam is sitting on my high stool by the podium. He is dangling his rather large feet and swinging them a little. He is furiously taking notes as well.

My lesson is suddenly interrupted by Susan. "You know, Mrs. Sprenger, it isn't fair!"

The surprise shows on my face and I quickly retort, "What isn't fair, Susan?"

"It isn't fair that Nicky and Katie are walking around and we have to sit down!"

Now I am truly surprised. These students have been walking in the back of my room for months. Katie is a good friend of Susan's. Why would she suddenly be concerned about this?

"I'm sorry, Susan. I try to meet the learning needs of all of my students. If you have the desire to get up and walk quietly as these two are, please feel free to do that."

Susan looks around at her classmates. No one else is objecting to the two students' movements, but Susan has a need to take advantage of my offer. She rises and walks to the back of the room.

I continue my discussion about the war. Katie and Nick are participating as they move about. Susan walks back and forth three times. She then returns to her seat.

SAMENESS IS NOT ALWAYS FAIRNESS

The first thing my students learn in my classroom is that I will do all that I can to assist in their learning experience. I want their needs to be met and their comfort level to be such that learning can take place. I have no intention of wasting their time or mine. The next thing they learn is that everyone's needs are different, and that treating all students the same is not always fair. This is a concept that is difficult for early adolescents, and that difficulty sometimes continues throughout high school.

The fact is that Katie and Nick learn better if they are allowed to move. Adam also likes to move, but if he is allowed to sit up high and dangle his feet, that will provide enough movement for him. Katie, Nick, and Adam are three very bright children. But I didn't always feel that way about them. Actually, in many ways, I would once have described them as disasters! They were often fooling around and moving at their desks so much that they drove me crazy! Many of the students in their class also were bothered by their behavior, so they were grateful when I created a way for their movement to be more controlled.

Kinesthetic Memory and the Semantic Lane

The subgroups of kinesthetic learners may respond differently to different memory lanes. We have doodlers, whole-body learners, hands-on learners, and we may at times deal with a kinesthetic learner whose brain is turned on through emotion. This internal aspect of kinesthetic activity is visible in the learner who slumps down in the chair and generally looks comfortable—usually too comfortable looking for us visual teachers. We constantly ask them to "sit up straight," which they can do for a few minutes and then return to their previous comfy state. We should ask these students a question to see if they indeed are on task. If they are, allow them to sit comfortably, as it will help them learn.

In general, we can say that most of these subtypes have one thing in common: When it comes to semantics, the textbook and reading are not priorities. Remember that semantic information must go through a short-term process before it can be stored in long-term memory. Somehow through movement those words need to be processed.

For the doodler, the solution might be

- Mind mapping
- Story mapping
- Webbing
- Drawing

For the hands-on learner we could try

- Math manipulatives
- Building
- Dioramas
- Clay
- Role play

- Playing cards with information on them (like the game "Go Fish" with matching facts or complementary ideas)

The whole-body learner could benefit from

- Role playing
- Body mapping
- "Walking through an essay" (Have the components of an essay outlined on the floor with masking tape. Students walk from the introduction to the body paragraphs and then to the conclusion.)
- "Walking through a math problem" (Create a calculator on the floor with masking tape; step from numeral to numeral and figure out the answer.)
- Putting information in different corners of the room; have students walk to each area and read or discuss the information.
- Signs in the room above the board that say "Agree" and "Disagree"; when discussing controversial issues have students rise and stand in a row in front of the opinion they choose.
- Adding tastes and smells to the learning when possible
- Mnemonic devices that require movement and body integration, like a body peg system or an acrostic that requires finger motions
- Having this learner follow along with his or her finger while reading
- Tracing letters and words for spelling and to remember facts
- Using computer technology to allow movement while learning
- Creating puzzles
- Learning centers—it doesn't matter what grade you teach!

Kinesthetic Memory and the Episodic Lane

This memory lane deals with location and events. For the kinesthetic learner who requires hands-on activities and movement, how can we provide an environment that is memorable and moveable? Here are some suggestions:

- Field trips—especially those that allow exploration and interaction
- Pull-down maps and pictures
- Globes
- Seat changes to specific locations so this memory can still be used for assessment (Random moves may cause some episodic memory to be lost.)
- Specific seating arrangements that the students can create themselves: an arrangement for listening to book reports, an

arrangement for cooperative groups, an arrangement for viewing video clips, and an arrangement for computer access. Have the students move the furniture around for the different learning experiences. It will allow them movement and help them create some mental images of their learning space.

- Have students bring in "action figures" to represent some of the learning. These can be used for role play.
- Hang different-colored paper in the room representing different concepts or ideas. Let students combine the papers as they associate the ideas.
- Provide a "touchable" environment that matches your current area of study.

Tony's high school classroom is located next to the band room. For several of his English classes, he and his students are "serenaded" by blossoming musicians. It drives the auditory learners crazy! With no success in changing rooms, Tony sends home a newsletter asking for old carpeting. His plan is to carpet the wall adjacent to the band room and muffle the tones. Much to his pleasure and surprise, one of the parents works at a carpet store. An order had come in and one entire roll of carpet was streaked! The store offers to give Tony the carpet. Even better, the carpet is light beige and will not darken the room.

On a Saturday afternoon, Tony and a few of his students hang the carpet. One particular student, Calvin, can't keep from rubbing his hands over the carpet. As Tony observes, he finds Calvin to be extremely kinesthetic/tactile. He touches everything!

From a workshop Tony attended on brain-based teaching, he has been using a strategy called "The Knowledge Wall." This strategy allows students to put note cards with information such as formulas up on a wall and, with permission, during a classroom assessment they may go up to the wall and read the "knowledge" written there. They are not allowed to write anything down until they get back to their seats. Calvin often raises his hand and goes to the wall, but he doesn't seem able to retain the information long enough to get it on paper.

Tony decides to make the carpeted wall the new "Knowledge Wall." He is hopeful that Calvin and other learners like him will benefit from the tactile experience along with the information on the cards. As he suspects, as Calvin approaches the wall to gain insight, he rubs and manipulates the carpet in his fingers. Calvin's scores start to rise. Tony finds that several others in his classrooms benefit in the same way!

Some teachers have had the opportunity to put an exercise bike in their classrooms. These were quiet bikes that students were allowed to ride and read. Of course, every student wants a turn on the bike, but the truly kinesthetic learner benefits most from the activity. In fact, the auditory learners found that even the quietest bike makes some noise, and they were often distracted. Some visual learners found that there was too much movement of the text and found that distracting. The learners with a strong need to move found it helpful in focusing on the material. Some also said that during assessments, they could look at the bicycle and remember what they read while riding. Truly kinesthetic memory through the episodic lane!

Kinesthetic Memory and the Procedural Lane

This combination appears to be a natural. But it's not quite that simple. Just because some enjoy and even require movement, doesn't mean that their procedural memory is strong. Procedural memory requires repetition of exact steps to the point of automaticity. There are kinesthetic learners who have a great deal of trouble with procedural memory. As noted in the previous chapter, according to Ruby Payne (1998), most students from generational poverty lack procedural memory skills. As a result, they often don't finish assignments or projects because they don't follow through. One way to get them started on procedures is to have them plan a classroom party. As they do so, they must write down each step. The party is the celebration of completing their procedural memory task!

Since kinesthetic students are usually quite aware of their bodies, movement, sports, and dance may be second nature to them. These students may even be able to create and teach motor procedures to other students. For the auditory and visual learners who are very weak in this area, forming groups with the movers and shakers as leaders may be fun for all and make these often misunderstood learners (kinesthetic) feel important. Using kinesthetic memory via the procedural motor pathway may include using the following strategies:

Figure 6.1   The Civil War Games

- Dance—creative movement can express ideas, concepts, and processes
- Measuring using body parts
- Demonstrations of labs
- Sports metaphors—comparing wars and battles to football: What does the ball represent? The end zone? The quarterback?
- Gymnastics
- Computer drill
- Creating games using unit material
- Charades

For nonmotor procedural memories made through the kinesthetic pathway, you will find that repetition is going to be necessary. Without repetition, this learner may not get a picture of what a proper heading is for a paper. It will be extremely helpful if all teachers use the same heading format. In that way, the "mental picture" of what the learner is to do will come more quickly and with less confusion. The same can be said for such procedures as letter writing. Grammar rules for capitalization and punctuation take drill with reinforcement, like Daily Oral Language (Putting sentences on the board or overhead and having students make either oral or written corrections). I tweaked my grammar program and made it extremely helpful in this area, as my students had several initial weeks of correcting sentences and placing a rule number by the correction. This forced the students to read the rules until most of them were in long-term memory.

Other step-by-step procedures can be written on individual index cards. The student can manipulate the cards and try to put them in the correct order.

Kinesthetic Memory and Conditioned Response

It is quite possible that students with a strong kinesthetic preference, like the auditory learners, may have musical talent. Holding and playing an instrument can provide a wonderful outlet and a way to turn on their brains.

For the conditioned response lane through the kinesthetic memory pathway, the students may

- Create songs and/or music
- Create raps with movement
- Play games that require rapid answers using a ball or bean bag toss to the question recipient
- Use flash cards
- Do computer drills
- Create metaphors with movement
- Do "high fives" for correct answers—this encourages correct responses and gives the student an immediate kinesthetic response to help memory (If you are comfortable with your students, you can do "low" fives for incorrect or close answers, too.)
- Create cheers with posters (See Figure 6.2)

Kinesthetic Memory and the Emotional Lane

"I just felt like doing it." Our feelings often guide our behavior. Kinesthetic learners who have a strong internal need to process feelings may be able to create powerful emotional memories. Unfortunately for them, our educational system doesn't support or measure these memories. Our accountability is measured through semantic pathways. This truth affects all of our students, but it seems that the kinesthetic learner has the most difficulty with the school structure.

Adding emotions to kinesthetic learning might include the following:

- Acting out stories with strong emotional implications
- Debate

Figure 6.2   Cheer With Posters

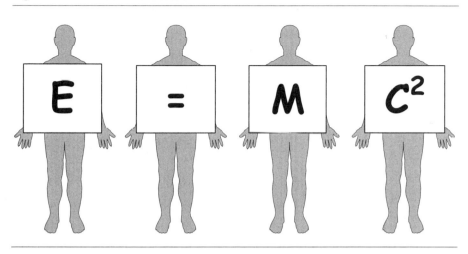

- Dance
- Role play
- Modeling your enthusiasm
- Charades
- Being part of a team

The trial and error approach to learning is powerful (Gully, Payne, Koles, & Whiteman, 2002). As our brains process our attempts, they also learn to avoid what doesn't work. I always tell my students that Thomas Edison found about 999 ways *not* to invent the light bulb! It was through trials and tribulations that many of our greatest inventions came about. This type of learning easily stores information in long-term memory, and part of that memory are the emotions involved with it: curiosity, excitement, disappointment, anger, frustration, and success.

DOES IT REALLY MAKE ANY DIFFERENCE?

This is a question I get quite often. It is usually followed by, "These kids don't really learn that way. They just can't focus." I feel like the perfect person for this question. I live with two kinesthetic learners. As I mentioned earlier, my husband, Scott, is a hands-on learner. Marnie, my daughter, is a mover and shaker. She really needs to move. I can prove it.

In third grade, Marnie was chosen to be tested for our "gifted" school. It is rare that an entire school is devoted to gifted children, but in our district this is offered. To be tested, I had to take Marnie to a local university testing service. Marnie's test was a disaster. She was tested by an elderly gentleman. He was from the "old" school. He believed that children should sit still and listen. As I waited outside the door, I could hear the conversation. I cringed. The examiner kept telling Marnie to sit down. His agitation was evident by the end of the oral test.

She couldn't wait to get out of the building. I was unhappy with the experience for her. We waited for the test results. They were not awful, but they were not good enough for acceptance to the school. I am usually not a pushy parent. But this time . . .

I called the principal of the gifted school and told him of the experience. He offered to have her tested again. I called the university and asked about the examiners. There was only one other examiner. I called her and asked if she would allow Marnie to move around while she answered the questions. The woman said it would be no problem and that others before had done so. Marnie's score—and I realize this is an arbitrary test—was over 20 points higher! She attended the gifted school. The reason I wanted Marnie in this school was because they offered more real-world problem solving, more field trips, and in general, more opportunities for movement.

So, my answer is, "Yes. It makes a difference!"

KINESTHETIC MEMORY: I'D RATHER DO IT MYSELF!

Students with a strong kinesthetic preference know that they are well coordinated, have athletic ability, and they generally reinforce their learning through a sense of touch. They often feel good about their bodies. Creating rubrics for the following types of products may be tricky. Determining with students what the critical features of their products are may help them understand what you are expecting and what they can create. Choices to give them for assessments might include:

- Drama
- Dance
- Building a model
- Sculpting
- Performing an experiment
- Gymnastics
- Computer presentations
- Diorama
- Pantomime

Many of these learners have difficulty in school due to their lack of visualization skills. I have found that videotaping their performances and allowing them to watch themselves often enable them to "see" what they are doing. This may make switching to visual learning and visualization, which we do so much of in school, easier.

BLOOM'S TAXONOMY AND THE KINESTHETIC LEARNER

The following defines again each level of thinking in Bloom's taxonomy (1956). The kinesthetic learner should be encouraged to think at each of these levels.

- *Knowledge:* recalling facts, terms, definitions, and basic concepts

- *Comprehension:* organizing, comparing, translating, interpreting, giving descriptions, and stating main ideas to demonstrate understanding

- *Application:* applying acquired knowledge, facts, techniques, and rules in a way to solve problems

- *Analysis:* breaking information into its parts by identifying motives or causes; making inferences and finding evidence to support generalizations. Categorization is one way to reorganize information to show analysis.

- *Synthesis:* compiling information in a different way by uniting elements in a new pattern or suggesting alternative solutions

- *Evaluation:* based on a set of criteria, presenting and defending opinions by making judgments about information, validity of ideas, or quality of work

Encouraging critical thinking in our kinesthetic students will not be a problem if they have been instructed in the style that fits them. Applying higher-level thinking becomes easier once you have something to think about!

An interesting approach to kinesthetic learning for all students involves *kinesthetic imagination* (Patterson, 1997). Athletes often imagine themselves involved in their sport, and because there is an area in the brain for this practice, they actually can improve their performance. Since we all have this capability, students can imagine themselves doing something that may lead to higher-level thinking. This process will also involve visualization and some verbal processing. As you look at the words involved in each taxonomy level, think of ways your students could use their kinesthetic imaginations. For instance, in the Synthesis section you could suggest, "Using your kinesthetic imagination, create a different approach Hercules could have taken with Zeus." From this kinesthetic approach using visualization, the student may find it easier to write or talk about the lesson.

Knowledge

Words to use for this level include:

Omit	Define	Name
Where	Label	Relate
Which	Show	Tell
Choose	Spell	Recall
Find	List	Select
How	Match	

Some possible questions include:

How would you demonstrate . . . ?

Match the information on the cards to . . .

Select the appropriate tools . . .

On the computer, define . . .

Comprehension

Words to use for this level include:

Compare	Extend	Translate
Contrast	Illustrate	Summarize
Demonstrate	Infer	Show
Interpret	Outline	Classify
Explain	Relate	

Some possible questions include:

Through physical interpretation, summarize . . .

Using any medium, illustrate . . .

Use a model to show . . .

Translate these words into movement . . .

With some classmates, create a human illustration of . . .

Application

Words to use for this level include:

Apply	Make use of	Solve
Build	Organize	Utilize
Choose	Experiment with	Model
Construct	Plan	Identify
Develop	Select	

Some possible questions include:

Make use of the_____in your own application of . . .

Experiment with the . . . (plan, formula, idea).

Through trial and error, solve . . .

Model the appropriate . . .

Analysis

Words to use for this level include:

Analyze	Examine	Theme
Categorize	Inspect	Relationships
Classify	Simplify	Function
Compare	Survey	Motive
Contrast	Take part in	Inference
Discover	Test for	Assumption
Dissect	Distinguish	Conclusion
Divide	List	

Some possible questions include:

Create a model comparing and contrasting . . .

Perform a skit in which you show the relationships between or among . . .

Recreate the theme through a dance . . .

Categorize the feelings (facts, ideas) found on the cards before you.

Synthesis

Words to use for this level include:

Build	Imagine	Change
Choose	Invent	Adapt
Combine	Make up	Minimize
Compile	Originate	Maximize
Compose	Plan	Delete
Construct	Predict	Theorize
Create	Propose	Elaborate
Design	Solve	Test
Develop	Suppose	Improve
Estimate	Discuss	Happen
Formulate	Modify	Change

Some possible questions include:

Build a model to solve . . .

Imagine and design a structure . . .

Invent a _____ to solve . . .

Test the theory . . .

What could be done to improve . . . ?

Evaluation

Words to use for this level include:

Award	Measure	Support
Choose	Compare	Prove
Conclude	Mark	Disprove
Criticize	Rate	Assess
Decide	Recommend	Influence
Defend	Select	Perceive
Determine	Agree	Value
Dispute	Interpret	Estimate
Evaluate	Explain	Deduct
Judge	Appraise	
Justify	Prioritize	

Some possible questions include:

Measure, compare, and interpret your findings . . .

Prove or disprove _____ through any means.

Demonstrate your evaluation of . . .

Justify your support of_____ using a model.

It is not a simple task to develop higher-level thinking through hands-on and movement strategies. According to Dr. Jay Giedd at the National Institute of Health, recent research suggests strongly that we encourage movement in our students to promote learning. The structures in the brain that navigate our thought processes work better with movement (Spinks, 2002). Offer students the opportunity to create their own higher-level questions and tasks. In order to do this successfully, they must be familiar with the material, hold it in working memory, and use synthesis and evaluation to determine what assignments are doable.

THE CRITTER CONNECTION

The kinesthetic child has the most difficulty in any traditional classroom. The problem is that the brain is not turned on without movement or touch. If their learning preference is not honored, they become stuck in an area of the brain where no learning takes place. When Marnie found herself in classrooms where movement was not appropriate, she simply spaced out and daydreamed through her classes. Of course, her grade point suffered as well as her class rank. She was labeled "bright, but lazy" by many teachers. There had to be an answer for Marnie and others like her.

I felt there needed to be a better answer for everyone. You see, I could share this information and some teachers would allow their kinesthetic students the freedom to walk around the classroom while they spoke. However, other teachers were too easily distracted by that movement. I also often suggest that teachers allow these students to stand at their desks, perhaps with one knee on the chair. Again, some teachers could tolerate this type of freedom for their students, and others could not.

The kinesthetic student responds well to touch. We have encouraged teachers and parents to place a hand on a shoulder or arm of a kinesthetic student to get his or her attention and activate the brain. This is met with much approval. The only drawback is the number of students in the room who need this attention and the speed at which the student goes "off task" when the adult walks away.

Sometimes proximity is useful. The teacher being close to the student without touching may keep the child on task for a period of time. Yet, staying within the proper range is challenging in most classrooms (close enough to benefit the student; far enough away to keep him comfortable).

In my research on the need for touch, an idea began to develop. I started gradually bringing stuffed animals into the classroom to provide a feeling of security and belonging to the room atmosphere. There were times when the students were handed the animals to hold and pet. These students appeared to calm down and pay attention while handling the "critters," as they were fondly labeled. I discovered that several interesting problems were solved by the critters:

1. Students calmed down by stroking the critters.

2. When students had the critters, they disrupted other students less frequently.

3. Students who were not kinesthetic but were having a bad day were soothed by holding the critters.

Figure 6.3

Critter Credentials

I, _____ , agree to the care and feeding
   name of adoptive parent

of my "Study Buddy" during my _____class.

_____
                  Signature   Date

---

4. Unlike clicking pens, banging fists, tapping rulers, and opening and closing books, the critters made no noise, so those sensitive to sound were not distracted.

5. Students felt a bonding with the teacher because they could have their own "pet."

6. Many high school teachers adopted this strategy. They were not surprised to find that teenagers also like to hold the critters, particularly when their "emotional roller coaster" is out of control!

7. Students who were allowed to "adopt" a critter, which included signing papers and naming it, were more attached to and more soothed by the critters.

DIFFERENT STROKES

1. All Learners Need Differentiation

I started my teaching career in the room next to Donna. We were teaching at a middle school. One year the principal wanted to "group" the students in Language Arts. I got the "high" group, and Donna took the "low" group. We both faced challenges as never before. She found many of her students to be kinesthetic learners who were lagging behind because their brains just hadn't been "turned on." Donna took her students out of the classroom quite often. In nice weather, they went outside and role played stories, created scenarios that they acted out or mimed, and did several hands-on problem-solving activities. Although my group assumed they were the "smart" ones, many of them asked to be placed in Donna's class. They didn't want to miss out on the fun. Plus some of my "gifted" students were also kinesthetic, and they wanted to move. I changed my strategies for my class and began our own "road trips" to the playground and field. One particular project involved creating a myth, writing a script for it, designing costumes, and making a video. For the 1970s, this was high tech, and the students loved it. If I learned nothing else that year, I learned the importance of every teacher having knowledge of both gifted and special needs strategies.

2. Rug Rats

When I give workshops, I am always impressed with the creativity and abundance of ideas my colleagues contribute. One high school teacher did something wonderful for her kinesthetic learners. She went to a carpet store that was closing and volunteered to take all of their small square carpet samples. These fit nicely on the floor beneath the students' desks. They could then take off their shoes and rub their feet on the carpet. Many kinesthetic learners took advantage of this and would often come to her room to borrow carpet for another classroom assessment.

3. Learning Is in the Bag!

A small bean bag may just do the trick for your kinesthetic student. Bean bags can be purchased or easily made. If you opt to make your own, try for the brain-compatible colors of sky blue or pink. For material, you could use felt, velveteen, velour, or terrycloth. The movement of the beans inside creates a calming effect and a feeling of large-muscle movement.

4. Pushing the Right Buttons!

A fabric-covered button may give your student the stimulation he needs to turn on that brain. A large button may be preferable to a small one, especially if this child likes to put things in his mouth. (Kinesthetics often do!) Velvet buttons are usually available at fabric stores. You may also make your own buttons. I have seen felt stick-ons available in many colors. Corduroy and terrycloth are two fabrics that kinesthetics often like.

5. Knowing Their Place!

Many students enjoy working on their beds. You know the ones who are all sprawled out on the bedspread with work everywhere? The motivation for this is the texture of the bedspread or blanket. These students love that stimulation. So how about giving it to them in the classroom? Find a placemat that is the texture your students prefer. Let them put it on their desks and see how calming it is as they rub the fabric. (Teachers, this may be a great art project for the whole class. Get some fabric and personalize "learning mats"!)

6. Exercises

Many teachers are using exercises throughout the day for their kinesthetic learners as well as all students who need to get some blood circulating. *Brain Gym* activities, designed by Dr. Paul Dennison (Dennison & Dennison, 1994), are popular and easy to use. This is a controlled way of allowing students the movement they require and enhancing whole-brain learning.

Putting It All Together

7

"I was teaching my students about the brain today, and it dawned on me—memory CREEPS in!" Janice announces.

"At my age, it just creeps out!" Margo replies.

"No, C-R-E-E-P-S," Janice insists. "CR is for Conditioned Response, E is for Emotional, the next E is for Episodic, P is for Procedural, and S is for Semantic. I gave them an acronym to help them remember the memory lanes. Do you like it?" she asks.

"I'll be happy to steal that idea!" I respond. "In fact, let's take it a step farther. Let's create a profile chart for us and for the kids to see how they learn."

"You mean VAK and then CREEPS?" Janice asks.

"Exactly. We can have a chart for each student. It will be helpful if the student is having trouble. And we'll be able to see if our instruction and assessment are matching their needs," I add.

"Let's make this simple. I already have a ton of paperwork to do," Margo interjects.

"Not only will it be simple, but the students can work on it as well!" I respond.

"Let's get started on this," Janice says excitedly. "I think it's going to be helpful. We could even send it with the students next year in their portfolios. It will feel a little less like starting over if we have this kind of information at the beginning of the year."

We worked together on this project and came up with the profile chart in Figure 7.1 to give to students.

The student's name will go in the upper left corner. Across the top are the three sensory pathways. Those will go in according to each student's pattern (VAK, VKA, AKV, AVK, KVA, KAV). Down the left side are the five memory pathways. The following sample, Figure 7.1, is a generic chart filled in with possible ideas for each learning strength and memory lane. Students will personalize their charts with your help. They can keep track of strategies that work for them or that they want to try.

IDENTIFYING LEARNING STRENGTHS

The next step was to help our students identify their learning strengths. There are several ways to do this. Observation, student conference, and the test included in Chapter 2 are all possibilities. There are also two other options—if you are willing to take the chance!

I call this a POP test. That stands for Passing Out Papers, and it goes like this:

1. Discover in the first few days who the movers and shakers are. They cannot help but present themselves.

2. Choose the child who needs to move the most. (The one who gets to the pencil sharpener and discovers he has a marker in his hand instead of a pencil.)

3. Give the student a stack of papers and ask him to pass out one to each student. He cannot give the papers to the first person in a row or on a team. He must personally hand each classmate a sheet. (Realize that you have just made his dreams come true!)

4. As the student passes out the papers, he will undoubtedly need to make some physical impression on his fellow classmates. He may push, shove, pinch, or move objects on their desks.

5. As this process is taking place, have your grade book or a sheet with the students' names in your hand—and a pencil in the other hand.

6. Observe the reaction of each student to this kinesthetic learner. Here are examples of the types of behavior you might expect to see:

   (a) The visual learners will roll their eyes or give him a dirty look.
   (b) The auditory learner will have something to say to him.

Figure 7.1

Lesson/Unit:	VISUAL	AUDITORY	KINESTHETIC
C.conditioned R.esponse	Flash cards Poetry with drawings	Jingles Repetition–tape recorder	Rap with movement Cheers Snap, Krackle, Pop
E.pisodic	Posters/bulletin boards Field trips	Sounds: music, chimes Field trips	"Walk around the room" Field trips
E.motional	Draw pictures Write stories	Tell stories Role play	Role play Dance
P.rocedural	Picture steps Written steps	Tape record Talk through	Demonstration Experiment Manipulatives
S.emantic	Mind map with symbols Overhead White board Textbook	Small-group discussion Information on audiotape Read aloud	Charades Drama Walk while reading Work at chalk or white board

(c) The kinesthetic learners will be moving or touching him as he goes by.

7. Quickly mark V, A, or K next to the students' names.

This little experiment gives fairly accurate results; however, I suggested a pencil because you may find as time goes by that the preference is different than you recorded.

If you want another "sampling," you can try the following procedure:

1. Tell your students that they must sit quietly for five minutes. No reading, no talking, no moving around.

2. Simply sit and observe. In a matter of one or two minutes you may see the following behaviors:

(a) Visual learners will look around and absorb or read everything they see.

(b) Auditory learners will mumble to themselves.

(c) Kinesthetic learners will fidget, get out a piece of paper for doodling, or slump down comfortably in their seats.

I don't find the "quiet" test to be nearly as much fun or as accurate as the "POP" test, but many teachers like it.

A CLOSER LOOK

In order to give you a clearer understanding of the learning and memory profile chart, I am including profile charts for some of the students you've met in this book. On their charts, the learning strength comes first, their secondary preference is next, and then the modality they are most uncomfortable with. I have made suggestions of specific strategies for their strength in each memory lane. Then I have added a few suggestions in the other sensory pathways to help them stretch and transfer information.

In Chapter 2, you met Jeffrey and Elise. Jordan is the student with weak visual memory skills in Chapter 4, while Isaac, Micayla, and Tobias are students with visual preferences discussed in the same chapter. Chapter 5 brought us Lemar, Amos, and Amanda, who have auditory strengths. In Chapter 6, we met Calvin, a strong kinesthetic learner.

Jeffrey

Jeffrey is a visual learner who is rather independent. I have filled in possible visual strategies for him in each memory lane for the Visual

Figure 7.2

Lesson/Unit Jeffrey	VISUAL	AUDITORY	KINESTHETIC
C.onditioned R.esponse	Flash cards	Rap	
E.pisodic	Unique environment		
E.motional	Write stories	Tell stories	
Procedural	Write procedures step by step		Manipulatives
S.emantic	Mind map with symbols		Charades

135

column. I would expect him then to be able to stretch himself first into the auditory and then the kinesthetic areas. I have placed suggestions in a few of the categories. He would rather work by himself, so for his emotional intelligence and the emotional atmosphere of the room I would want him to begin interacting with others. Visually, he will understand the material. Once it is mastered, the discomfort of stretching won't be hindered by doubts about the material. (See Figure 7.2.)

Elise

Elise likes to interact with others as she moves. She is therefore Kinesthetic-Auditory-Visual. As her weakest area appears to be visual, I would like to see her work in that area after she feels comfortable with the unit work. The auditory pathway for her is probably easily accessible once she starts moving and interacting through her kinesthetic channel. Episodically, offering a field trip for this student will satisfy the visual, auditory, and kinesthetic areas. (See Figure 7.3.)

Jordan

This kinesthetic learner needs to work on his visual memory. To begin, information needs to be learned through his kinesthetic pathway. Therefore, I have a strategy for each memory lane in that pathway. Once that is accomplished, Jordan can begin working on first auditory and then visual memory. Since he is most sensitive to and uncomfortable with visual, I would offer repetitive visual experiences until he feels more comfortable with his visual memory. (See Figure 7.4.)

Isaac

Isaac remembered his test information by seeing me in the spot where I gave him the information. This student relies on his visual episodic memory. He has a strong visual preference, as we witnessed when he was taking his test. Since Isaac must learn to apply his knowledge outside the location where he learned it, I need to help him use other memory lanes and stretch outside his visual strength. In that way, he will learn triggers for his memory other than locations and people (invisible information). (See Figure 7.5.)

Micayla

This young student was having difficulty with procedures that weren't written down. Her head was "spinning" as I gave directions orally.

(Text continues on page 140)

Figure 7.3

Lesson/Unit			
Elise	**KINESTHETIC**	**AUDITORY**	**VISUAL**
C.conditioned R.esponse	Cheers	Rap	
E.pisodic	Touchable		Field trips
E.motional	Drama		Drawing
P.rocedural	Engaged learning (computer)		
S.emantic	Peer teaching		Mind mapping

Figure 7.4

Lesson/Unit			
Jordan	*KINESTHETIC*	*AUDITORY*	*VISUAL*
C.onditioned R.esponse	Snap, Krackle, Pop	Rap	
E.pisodic	Walking from place to place		Creating visuals for the bulletin board
E.motional	Acting	Interviewing	Drawing pictures or creating collages
P.rocedural	Demonstration		
S.emantic	Walk and talk		Mind mapping

Figure 7.5

Lesson/Unit			
Isaac	*VISUAL*	*KINESTHETIC*	*AUDITORY*
C.onditioned R.esponse	Poetry with drawings	Rap	Metaphor
E.pisodic	Posters		
E.motional	Writing poetry	Drama	
P.rocedural	Steps that rhyme		
S.emantic	Textbook; graphic organizers	Role play	Interview

139

Auditory information is the most difficult for Micayla. It is important to make her feel confident in her visual pathway, and then give her as much time as she needs to practice with her auditory memory. As we go through life, there are many occasions when we must be able to remember some simple steps or instructions that we receive verbally. Micayla needs to practice with her auditory active working memory. (See Figure 7.6.)

Tobias

Tobias learns best through his visual pathway. Graphic organizers that create pictures of the material in his mind will make his semantic learning easier. To stretch Tobias, I must get him to verbally share information. For that reason, I have chosen rap, storytelling, and peer teaching. These activities can occur after he is confident he knows the information through his visual pathway and probably through his kinesthetic pathway as well. According to Levine (2002), motor activity can improve active working memory. Therefore, the kinesthetic activities may help Tobias "hold onto" auditory information and give him the ability to share verbally. (See Figure 7.7.)

Lemar

Lemar is a student from poverty. He is a kinesthetic learner, but as a result of feeling inadequate at understanding verbal directions for a kinesthetic activity, he turned to the auditory pathway to succeed. He has a problem with auditory procedural memory. On Lemar's profile, I have included both kinesthetic and auditory suggestions. I think he will benefit from both. Since auditory is his second preference, he will have some options in case he feels "dumb" in a situation. Then it will be time to stretch him to the visual arena. If his procedural memory problems extend to his ability to give information in order, reading and listening to stories may provide him with the patterns he needs to follow. (See Figure 7.8.)

Amos

His strong auditory preference creates sound sensitivity for Amos. He will learn most easily through listening and speaking. It is important that Amos interact with the kinesthetic and visual world as well. He is already a good student, so convincing him of this necessity may take some time. I would use the "one picture is worth a thousand words" adage with Amos. He should be able to make the stretch to visual quite easily. If he remains unsure of his kinesthetic ability, that may take more time. (See Figure 7.9.)

(Text continues on page 144)

Figure 7.6

Lesson/Unit	VISUAL	KINESTHETIC	AUDITORY
Micayla			
C.onditioned R.esponse	Reading repetition		Song lyrics
E.pisodic	Field trips		
E.motional	Writing poetry	Drama	
P.rocedural	Written steps	Practice at board	Oral repetition of written steps
S.emantic	Summarizing		Peer teaching

Figure 7.7

Lesson/Unit Tobias	VISUAL	KINESTHETIC	AUDITORY
C.onditioned R.esponse	Flash cards with pictures	Walk around the room	Rap
E.pisodic	Bulletin boards		Telling stories
E.motional	Stories/pictures/video	Charades	
P.rocedural	Steps with pictures	Models; experiments	
S.emantic	Graphic organizers		Peer teaching

142

Figure 7.8

Lesson/Unit			
Lemar	*KINESTHETIC*	*AUDITORY*	*VISUAL*
C.onditioned R.esponse	Clapping	Repetition – tape recorder	
E.pisodic	Touchable	Music	Drawings to go on bulletin board
E.motional	Role play	Debate	Read stories
P.rocedural	Walk through and record steps on tape	Tape recorder	
S.emantic	Models	Small-group discussion; listen to stories	Graphic organizers

Amanda

Amanda definitely needs to stretch to the visual pathway. Not seeing her jersey in the closet is a classic indicator of this problem. Since she is already showing a comfort level with kinesthetic memory through her activities, I can combine some auditory-kinesthetic strategies and then move her to visual memory with mind mapping and drawing. I particularly like mind mapping for Amanda because it combines both print and picture. She may favor one over the other as she begins to broaden her memory capabilities. (See Figure 7.10.)

Calvin

As Calvin's primary mode is kinesthetic, he had success with the Knowledge Wall when it became touchable. He could then hold the information that he read long enough to get it on paper. If visual memory is his second preference, combining some visual and auditory activities may help Calvin expand his active working memory for both. With his kinesthetic ability, working on an emotional level through debate and discussion may increase his auditory memory as well. (See Figure 7.11.)

AN EYE CUE

One of the most powerful nonverbal cues for cognitive processing involves the eyes. All learners' eyes will move according to the type of processing being done. Research in this area was initiated by Bandler and Grinder (1979), but several researchers support the theory (Jones, 2002; Payne, 1998). Being aware of eye movements can help us determine in which sensory pathway a student is processing. The information in Figure 7.12 pertains to eye movement patterns you would observe as you face most right-handed students.

Visual

If you are observing a right-handed student who is accessing remembered information, she will look up and to her left (your right). If the student is creating new information, she will look up to her right (your left). Left-handed students will do the opposite.

Auditory

If you are observing a right-handed student who is accessing remembered auditory information, she will look to her left side (your right).

(Text continues on page 148)

Figure 7.9

Lesson/Unit			
Amos	**AUDITORY**	**VISUAL**	**KINESTHETIC**
C.onditioned R.esponse	Rap		Adding movement to the rap
E.pisodic	Discussion of surroundings	Talking about posters	
E.motional	Debate		Creating a sports metaphor
P.rocedural	Oral repetition		
S.emantic	Small-group discussion/tape recorder with headset	Mind mapping in groups	Manipulatives

145

Figure 7.10

Lesson/Unit Amanda	AUDITORY	KINESTHETIC	VISUAL
C.onditioned R.esponse	Song lyrics	Rap	
E.pisodic	Theme music	Touchable environment	Drawing
E.motional	Drama		
P.rocedural	Say it/Do it		Writing out procedures from auditory memory
S.emantic	Read notes aloud into tape recorder and play back	Wipe off boards for problems	Mind mapping

Figure 7.11

Lesson/Unit			
CALVIN	**KINESTHETIC**	**VISUAL**	**AUDITORY**
C.onditioned R.esponse	Flash cards (tactile)		
E.pisodic	Touchable		
E.motional	Role playing		Debate
P.rocedural	Experiments; models		
S.emantic	Manipulatives; workbook	Mind mapping	Interviews Discussion

Figure 7.12

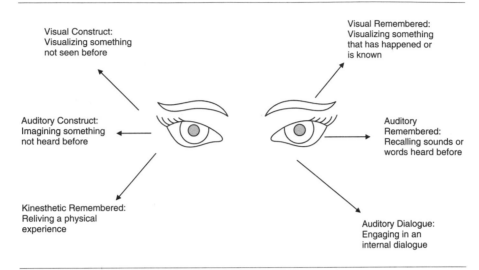

A right-handed student who is constructing new auditory information will look to her right side (your left). Left-handed students will do the opposite.

Kinesthetic

A right-handed student looking down to the left (your right) is accessing auditory internal dialogue. If she looks down to the right (your left), she is accessing her feelings. Left-handed students will do the opposite.

Gina storms into the room, throws her books on the floor, and slams herself into her desk. All eyes are on Margo as the students want to see how she will handle this. She walks over to Gina's desk, squats down, and quietly picks up her books. Gina is visibly upset.

Margo remains below Gina's eye level and quietly says, "You look pretty upset."

Gina looks down at Margo, and her tears start to fall. She begins explaining her anger. It has to do with not making the cut for the basketball team. Margo remains where she is until Gina finishes. When she is finished, Margo suggests that she go to the washroom and wipe her face. She may take someone with her if she chooses.

When she leaves, the students smile at Margo and get back on task.

One of the reasons the situation was diffused so quickly was Margo's physical position. Gina was upset and she wanted her to be able to express her feelings. Squatting to a level below Gina's eye level allowed her this access. Had she stood over her, Gina would have been accessing visual information and may have had difficulty expressing herself. This is one way eye accessing cues are helpful.

Julie is upset that she cannot find her homework. She knows that she did it, and she feels very silly not being able to remember where it is. She looks down with a red face.

"Julie, if you are trying to remember where you put it, look up and to your left," I suggest.

Julie looks at me funny, but she does as I ask. In a moment, she remembers. "I put it in my geography book!" She reaches in her book bag, pulls out the text, and finds her homework.

"How did you do that?" she asks me suspiciously.

"Teachers know everything!" I say with a chuckle.

Julie was upset with herself, which is why she was looking down. If Julie is a visual learner, she has to look up to access her information. Many times our students are embarrassed when they can't remember something, and as a result, they get into their feelings by looking down. They won't be able to access visually stored memory that way.

Encouragement is also a key here. If a student is looking to the side, he is trying to access auditory information. You can simply ask, "What do you remember hearing about that?" If a learner is looking down to his handedness, you can ask, "How do you feel about that?" The eye movements may be helpful in understanding how your students store and retrieve information (Payne, 1998).

"Eye cues" can also be applied to the position of peripherals in the classroom. The impact of visuals will vary according to their position. For instance, if you want stronger feelings induced, put visuals below eye level. Students will have to look down and get into their feelings. For information to be remembered, put content visuals above eye level, as this will aid with visual recall. To encourage discussion of information, put visuals at eye level for auditory access (Jensen, 2002).

REMEMBERING TO REMEMBER

Just as your students have learning strengths through a sensory pathway, they may also find that they have a memory strength. Determining their sensory strength is a bit easier than figuring out which memory lane works best for them. There are times when one lane will work for one kind of memory but doesn't work as well for other types of learning.

Here are some suggestions for helping your students discover their best memory profile:

1. Teach your students about how their memories work.

2. Explain that information learned in school will be useful outside of school.

3. To facilitate this "transfer," placing information in several memory lanes will be helpful. (Remind them that memory CREEPS in!)

4. Divide your students into five teams at the beginning of a new unit. Designate each team as a memory lane and let them choose a team name such as:

    (a) Conditioned Response: Jinglers
    (b) Episodic: Faces and Places
    (c) Emotional: Cry Babies
    (d) Procedural: Movers and Shakers
    (e) Semantic: Factoids

(1) Ask each group of students to take the current topic of study and find a way to place it in the memory lane their team is in charge of. For instance, the Episodic team might plan a field trip or create materials to decorate the room. Ask them to keep in mind the three sensory pathways as they do so. This allows team members with different learning strengths the opportunity to work on what is most comfortable as well as stretching to help others.

(2) Have students "teach" their team's information to the rest of the class to help them store it in their lane.

The results are wonderful. Each team has to cover the material in order to create a way to store it. Then each team "teaches" the other students, reinforcing the information again in their own minds. The material is repeated five different times and five different ways. According to Levine (2002), the best way to remember something is to change it in some way. All of the students will be doing this.

THINKING ABOUT THINKING

The metacognitive effects of this are great. Students begin to learn how they remember best. If you do the previous activity five times throughout the year, every student experiences storing information in each lane. The learners learn how they learn best. They can then choose to put information in all pathways or just their favorite.

Students will also learn the importance of the different memory lanes. Perhaps conditioned response is their favorite because they like to sing. They may discover that some concepts require more processing than just singing about them. They then will add a more appropriate way to remember that type of information.

DIFFERENT STROKES

Learning and Memory Tips for Students

- Intend to remember: Many times we forget because we didn't take the time to remember.
- Sleep on it! We encode memories while we sleep. When we have to study for a big test, it is best to study in short spurts followed by sleep. So study a bit each night, but only for a short time (Schenck, 2000).
- Try to associate what you are learning with something you already know. If the beetles you are studying in science will best be remembered by naming them John, Paul, George, and Ringo, use that connection!
- Be selective in what you are trying to remember. You may not have time to learn everything. Keep in mind who your audience will be.

In other words, if you are studying science and you know your science teacher loves vocabulary, be sure to remember those new words!

- Recite information aloud, even if auditory is not your strength. Walk while you say it, if movement is your strength. Write or draw while you say it if you are strong visually.

- Make mental pictures of what you are trying to remember. Again, this is good for all of us, no matter what our preferred sensory pathway may be.

- Forgetting and being "stupid" are not the same. Everyone forgets!

Epilogue

On the last day of the school year we meet at one of the neighborhood restaurants for dinner. The entire faculty and staff try to attend. We bring our significant others and celebrate the beginning of summer and some time to regroup for next year.

Scott and I join Margo, her husband Randy, Janice, and Tony at the end of the table. We make some small talk and order dinner.

"What are everyone's plans for the summer?" Margo asks. "I'm going to a conference in San Antonio on Brain-Based Teaching. The district is going to pay for part of it, and Randy is going with me. We figure it will be our vacation."

"I'm teaching workshops and graduate courses most of the summer. But I bet I'll see you in San Antonio," I reply.

"I'm teaching summer school," Tony chimes in. "As soon as I finish, Janice and I are going to Chicago for a conference on Differentiation. We think it will really help our teaching."

"I'm going to take a few classes this summer, too. I signed up for one on Learning and Memory and another on Matching Assessment and Instruction. They both sounded good and they fit in with my professional development plan," Janice adds.

Randy stands up and proclaims to the room, "Whoever said that teachers have their summers off just doesn't know the faculty at this school. I guess it's a good thing I'm not a teacher. I'm sure I would spend my summer fishing and sleeping!"

There is laughter, and several people nod in agreement.

"That's what I thought I would be doing when I started teaching. But you realize that you have to make hundreds of decisions each day, and in many ways the future of your students is in your hands. That's a pretty daunting realization," Tony declares.

Janice nods. "I learned so much this year, but I know I have to continue to add to the toolbox of strategies that I have. I want next year to be better, and I know I'll feel more confident if I continue to learn."

"It always does me good to spend my summers picking the brains of other teachers," I add. "Even though I'm teaching, I still get to steal lots of good ideas!"

We finish eating. Everyone prepares to leave. There are hugs and handshakes. We head out the door.

"Where did we park the car?" I ask Scott.

He just shakes his head and smiles. "You teach kids how to improve their learning and memory? Come on, Brainlady, I'll take you to the car."

I turn and look sheepishly at Margo and she says reassuringly, "Don't fret, my friend, I don't know where mine is either!"

Bibliography

Allen, R. (2002). *Impact teaching.* Boston: Allyn and Bacon.

Andreasen, N. (2001). *Brave new brain: Conquering mental illness in the era of the genome.* New York: Oxford University Press.

Armstrong, T. (1994). *Multiple intelligences in the classroom.* Alexandria, VA: Association for Supervision and Curriculum Development.

Atkinson, R., & Schiffrin, R. (1968). Human memory: A proposed system and its control processes. In K. T. Spence & J. W. Spence (Eds.), *The Psychology of Learning and Motivation: Vol 2.* New York: Academic Press.

Baddeley, A. (1999). *Essentials of human memory.* East Sussex, United Kingdom: Psychology Press.

Bandler, R., & Grinder, J. (1979). *Frogs into princes.* Moab, UT: Real People.

Bechara, A., Damasio, H., Damasio, A., & Lee, G. (1999). Different contributions of the human amygdala and ventromedial prefrontal cortex to decision-making. *Journal of Neuroscience, 19*(13), 5473–5481.

Bloom, B. S. (Ed.). (1956). *Taxonomy of educational objectives: The classification of educational goals: Handbook I, cognitive domain.* New York: Longmans, Green.

Blum, D. (1999). Attention deficit. *Mother Jones.* San Francisco: Foundation for National Progress. Retrieved from http://www.motherjones.com/mother_jones/JF99/Attentiondeficit.html

Boud, D., & Walker, D. (1991). *Experience and learning reflection at work.* Melbourne, Australia: Deakin University.

Bourtchouladze, R. (2002). *Memories are made of this.* London: Columbia University Press.

Burmark, L. (2002). *Visual literacy: Learn to see, see to learn.* Alexandria, VA: Association for Supervision and Curriculum Development.

Buzan, T. (2002). *Head first.* Bath, England: Bath Press Colourbooks.

Caine, G., & Caine, R. (1994). *Making connections: Teaching and the human brain.* New York: Innovative Learning.

Cowan, N. (2001). The magical number 4 in short-term memory: A reconsideration of mental storage capacity. *Behavioral and Brain Sciences, 24,* 87–114.

Dennison, P., & Dennison, G. (1994). *Brain gym.* Ventura, CA: Edu-Kinesthetics.

DePorter, B. (2000). *Discovering your personal learning style.* Oceanside, CA: Learning Forum.

Dunn, K., & Dunn, R. (1987). Dispelling outmoded beliefs about student learning. *Educational Leadership, 44*(6), 55–61.

Dye, L. (1999). *Humor on the brain.* Retrieved from http://abcnews.go.com/sections/science/DyeHard/dye990414.html

Geisel, T. (1992). *My many colored days.* New York: Knopf.

Giannetti, C., & Sagarese, M. (2001). *Cliques.* New York: Broadway Books.

Glasser, W. (1992). *The quality school.* New York: HarperCollins.

Glenn, H. S. (1990). *The greatest human need* [Video recording]. Gold River, CA: Capabilities.

Goleman, D. (1995). *Emotional intelligence.* New York: Bantam.

Goleman, D. (2002). *Primal leadership.* Boston: Harvard Business School Press.

Green, J. (2002). *The Green book of songs by subject: The thematic guide to popular music.* Nashville, TN: Professional Desk.

Green, J. (1993). *The word wall, teaching vocabulary through immersion.* Markham, Ontario, Canada: Pippin.

Gregory, G., & Chapman, C. (2002). *Differentiated instructional strategies.* Thousand Oaks, CA: Corwin.

Grinder, M. (1991). *Righting the educational conveyor belt.* Portland, OR: Metamorphous.

Guild, P., & Garger, S. (1998). *Marching to different drummers* (2nd ed.). Alexandria, VA: Association for Supervision and Curriculum Development.

Gully, S. M., Payne, S. C., Koles, K. L. K., & Whiteman, J. K. (2002). The impact of error-training and individual differences on training outcomes: An attribute-treatment interaction perspective, *Journal of Applied Psychology, 94*(1), 88–106.

Hannaford, C. (1995). *Smart moves.* Arlington, VA: Great Ocean.

Harmatz, M. B., Well, A. D., Overtree, C. E., Kawamura, K. Y., Rosal, M., & Ockene, I. S. (2000). Seasonal variation of depression and other moods: A longitudinal approach. *Journal of Biological Rhythms, 15*(4), 344–350.

Hathaway, W., Hargreaves, J., Thompson, G., & Novitsky, D. (1992). *A study into the effects of light on children of elementary school age.* Edmonton, Alberta, Canada: Alberta Education.

Hayes, E. (2002). *Remember the feeling: Emotional impact can be key to memory.* Retrieved from http://abcnews.go.com/sections/wnt/DailyNews/wnt_memory_a.html

Herschkowitz, N., & Herschkowitz, E. (2002). *A good start in life.* Washington, DC: Joseph Henry.

Heschong Mahone Group. (1999). *Daylighting in schools: An investigation into the relationship between daylight and human performance* (Condensed report). Retrieved from http://www.h-m-g.com/Daylighting/schoolc.pdf

Hopper, C. (2000). *Practicing college study skills* (2nd ed.). Boston: Houghton Mifflin.

Howard, P. (1999). *The owner's manual for the brain.* Austin, TX: Bard.

Jensen, E. (1998). *Teaching with the brain in mind.* Alexandria, VA: Association for Supervision and Curriculum Development.

Jensen, E. (2000a). *Music with the brain in mind.* San Diego, CA: The Brain Store.

Jensen, E. (2000b). *Learning with the body in mind.* San Diego, CA: The Brain Store.

Jensen, E. (2002). *Environments for learning.* San Diego, CA: The Brain Store.

Jensen, E., & Dabney, M. (2001). *Learning smarter.* San Diego, CA: The Brain Store.

Jones, C. (2002). *The source for brain-based learning.* East Moline, IL: LinguiSystems.

Keefe, J. M. (1997). *Instruction and the learning environment.* Larchmont, NY: Eye on Education.

Kessler, R. (2000). *The soul of education.* Alexandria, VA: Association for Supervision and Curriculum Development.

Kittredge, M. (1990). *The senses.* New York: Chelsea House.

Kline, P. (1997). *The everyday genius: Restoring children's natural joy of learning, and yours too.* Arlington, VA: Great Ocean.

Kosick, K. (Speaker). (2000). *Using brain research to reshape classroom practice* [Cassette recording]. Lynn, MA: Fleetwood Onsite Conference Recording.

LeDoux, J. (1996). *The emotional brain.* New York: Simon & Schuster.

LeDoux, J. (2002). *Synaptic self.* New York: Penguin.

Leiner, H., & Leiner, A. (1997, September). The treasure at the bottom of the brain. *The Brain Lab.* Retrieved from www.newhorizons.org/blab_leiner.html

Levine, M. (Speaker). (2000). *Memory factory tour* [Cassette recording]. Cambridge, MA: Educational Publishing Service.

Levine, M. (2002). *A mind at a time.* New York: Simon & Schuster.

Markova, D. (1992). *How your child is smart.* Emeryville, CA: Conari.

Markova, D., & Powell, A. (1998). *Learning unlimited.* Berkeley, CA: Conari.

Marshall, M. (2001). *Discipline without stress punishments or rewards.* Los Angeles: Piper.

Marzano, R. J., Pickering, D. J., & Pollack, J. E. (2001a). *Classroom instruction that works.* Alexandria, VA: Association for Supervision and Curriculum Development.

Marzano, R. J., Pickering, D. J., & Pollack, J. E. (2001b). *Handbook for classroom instruction that works.* Alexandria, VA: Association for Supervision and Curriculum Development.

Maslow, A., & Lowery, R. (Eds.). (1998). *Toward a psychology of being* (3rd ed.). New York: John Wiley.

McEwen, B., & Lasley, E. (2002). *The end of stress as we know it.* Washington, DC: Joseph Henry.

Meltzoff, A. (Speaker). (2000). Nurturing the young brain. *How the young brain learns* [Cassette recording]. Alexandria, VA: Association for Supervision and Curriculum Development.

Olivier, C., & Bowler, R. (1996). *Learning to learn.* New York: Fireside.

Patterson, M. N. (1997). *Every body can learn.* Tucson, AZ: Zephyr.

Payne, R. (1998). *A framework for understanding poverty.* Highlands, TX: aha! Process (formerly RFT Publishing).

Pease, B., & Pease, A. (2000). *Why men don't listen and women can't read maps.* New York: Welcome Rain.

Pert, Candace. (1997). *Molecules of emotion.* New York: Scribner.

Peterson, S. (Speaker). (2000). The nature of the young brain. *How the young brain learns* [Cassette recording]. Alexandria, VA: Association for Supervision and Curriculum Development.

Pike, R. (1994). *Creative training techniques handbook.* Minneapolis, MN: Lakeside.

Pike, R. (2001). *Guidelines for handouts.* Retrieved from http://www.bobpikegroup.com/support/free/deep/guideline.html

Ratey, J. (Speaker). (2000). *Care and feeding of the brain* [Cassette recording of presentation given at the Learning and the Brain conference]. Boston: Public Information Resources.

Restak, Richard. (2000). *Mysteries of the mind.* Washington, DC: National Geographic.

Rief, S. F. (1993). *How to reach and teach ADD/ADHD children: Practical techniques, strategies, and interventions for helping children with attention problems and hyperactivity.* San Francisco: Jossey-Bass.

Rose, C., & Nicholl, M. (1997). *Accelerated learning for the 21st century.* New York: Dell.

Schacter, D. (2001). *The seven sins of memory.* Boston: Houghton Mifflin.

Schenck, J. (2000). *Learning, teaching, and the brain: A practical guide for educators.* Thermopolis, WY: Knowabrain.

Seligman, M. (1995). *The optimistic child.* Boston: Houghton Mifflin.

Small, G. (2002). *The memory bible.* New York: Hyperion.

Society for Neuroscience. (2001, December). Humor, laughter and the brain. *Brain briefings.* Retrieved from http://apu.sfn.org/content/Publications/BrainBriefings/bb_humor.htm

Sousa, D. (Speaker). (2002). Is brain research making any difference in school? [Cassette recording of presentation given at the Summer Learning Brain Expo]. San Diego, CA: The Brain Store.

Spinks, S. (Producer). (2002, January 31). *Frontline: Inside the teenage brain* [Television broadcast]. Boston: Public Broadcasting Service.

Sprenger, M. (1999). *Learning and memory: The brain in action.* Alexandria, VA: Association for Supervision and Curriculum Development.

Sprenger, M. (2002). *Becoming a wiz at brain-based teaching.* Thousand Oaks, CA: Corwin Press.

Sprenger, M., & Posmer, G. (1997). *Powerfully simple techniques.* Peoria, IL: PST Publications.

Squire, L., & Kandel, E. (1999). *Memory: From mind to molecules.* New York: Scientific American Library.

Sylwester, R. (2000). *A biological brain in a cultural classroom.* Thousand Oaks, CA: Corwin Press.

Tileston, C. (2000). *Ten best teaching practices: How brain research, learning styles, and standards define teaching competencies.* Thousand Oaks, CA: Corwin Press.

Tomlinson, C. (1999). *The differentiated classroom: Responding to the needs of all learners.* Alexandria, VA: Association for Supervision and Curriculum Development.

Tomlinson, C. (Speaker). (2002). *Building a place to learn: Classroom environments and differentiated instruction* [Cassette recording]. Alexandria, VA: Association for Supervision and Curriculum Development.

Vygotsky, L. (1980). *Mind in society.* Cambridge, MA: Harvard University Press.

Wichmann, F., Lindsay, A., Sharpe, T., & Gegenfurtner, K.(2002). The contribution of color to recognition memory. *Journal of Experimental Psychology: Learning, Memory, and Cognition, 28*(3), 509–520.

Wilson, M. A., & McNaughton, B. L. (1994). Reactivation of hippocampal ensemble memories during sleep. *Science, 265,* 676–679.

Wolfe, P. (1996). The montillation of traxoline. *Mind, memory, and learning: Translating brain research to classroom practice* [Cassette manual]. Front Royal, VA: National Cassette Services.

Wolfe, P., Burkman, M., & Streng, K. (2000, March). The science of nutrition. *Educational Leadership, 57,* 54–59.

Zola, S. (Speaker). (2002). *Brain-based memory in the classroom* [Cassette recording of presentation given at the Summer Learning Brain Expo]. San Diego, CA: The Brain Store.

Index

**CORWIN
PRESS**

The Corwin Press logo—a raven striding across an open book—represents the happy union of courage and learning. We are a professional-level publisher of books and journals for K-12 educators, and we are committed to creating and providing resources that embody these qualities. Corwin's motto is "Success for All Learners."